REAL·HEI
OF WALES

Pub Interiors of Special Historic Interest

TAFARNAU·TREFTADAETH

Tafarnau o Ddiddordeb Hanesyddol Arbennig

Edited by **Michael Slaughter** and **Mike Dunn**

Photographs by Michael Slaughter LRPS

Project Co-ordinator Rhys Jones

Based on CAMRA's Inventory of Historic Pub Interiors in Wales

Produced by CAMRA's Pub Heritage Group
www.heritagepubs.org.uk
info.pubheritage@camra.org.uk
With support from CAMRA Books: Simon Hall, Katie Hunt and Emma Haines.

Published by the Campaign for Real Ale Ltd
230 Hatfield Road, St Albans, Hertfordshire AL1 4LW
www.camra.org.uk/books

ISBN 978-1-85249-275-5

A CIP catalogue record for this book is available from the British Library

Printed and bound in China by Kwong Fat Offset Printing Co., Ltd

Design/typography: Dale Tomlinson

Photographs © Michael Slaughter LRPS, apart from the following:
Page 65 (Ralph's label) – www.welshcider.co.uk
Page 65 (Cider glass) – Dave Matthews.
Page 15 (Blue Anchor, East Aberthaw exterior) – reproduced by kind permission of the owners
Page 54 (Douglas Arms, Bethesda exterior) – Gwyn Edwards
Page 100 (Fountain Inn at Troedrhiwgwair exterior) – Mike Dunn
Page 58 (Otley Beer Festival poster) – reproduced by kind permission of Otley Brewery

Acknowledgements
This guide builds on the work initially carried out by James 'Arfur' Daley and members of the CAMRA branches in South & Mid Wales. Our grateful thanks go to the members of all the CAMRA branches in Wales who have suggested candidates for inclusion.

The editors are very grateful to Rhys Jones for the enthusiastic way he has carried out the task of liaising with members of the CAMRA branches in Wales and also much appreciate the excellent help and support from Russ Durbridge, Keith Jenkins and David Lawrence; and to Geoff Brandwood for his helpful advice and proofreading.

Cover photography
Front: Red Lion, Dinas Mawddwy
Back: Cennen Arms, Trapp
Inside front: Mount Inn, Llanidloes
Inside back: Red Lion, Llansannan

Contents

Introduction

Features

Pub listings – Real Heritage Pubs of Wales

MANCHESTER UNITY
FRIENDLY SOCIETY
EARLY BIRD MENU
THE WATERLOO
7 COURSES

Introduction A Celebration of Welsh Pub Heritage

Real Heritage Pubs of Wales is a guide to a remarkable and varied collection of pubs with the best and most interesting interiors in the whole of Wales. It is CAMRA's pioneering initiative to bring greater appreciation of the most valuable historic pub interiors in the country to both local people and visitors. Although Wales has over 4,000 public houses, this guide lists just 100 or so. There are so few because of the enormous amount of opening out, theming and general modernisation that has taken place in recent decades. Safeguarding what is now left of the country's pub heritage has become a serious conservation challenge. By publishing this guide, we aim to encourage owners and local authorities to take steps to ensure that these surviving gems remain genuine historic pubs for years to come.

This guide builds on work started by CAMRA in the early 1990s to identify those pubs in the United Kingdom that still retained their historic interiors more or less intact. The result is the *National Inventory of Historic Pub Interiors,* details of which can be found by visiting www.heritagepubs.org.uk. Only 11 of the 288 pubs listed in the current inventory are in Wales (identified in this guide by ★ or ☆). The pubs included in this guide are very largely as they were before the mid-1960s (the start of a disastrous period of refitting pub interiors and opening out rooms) or, if they have been changed, this has been done sensitively and without destroying the historic heart. The survival of multiple rooms and old furnishings and fittings has been crucial to the selection. More information about CAMRA's project to save the nation's genuine historic pubs appears on page 28.

This guide to historic pub interiors in Wales contains a wide variety of pubs to visit, admire and enjoy. On pages 7–9 is a feature explaining the development of the pub from a simple beer house and revealing where it is still possible to drink in what looks like someone's front room! The Architectural Style in Welsh Pubs feature on pages 94–5 summarises the purpose-built pubs through the ages from the grand Victorian ones, through inter-war examples and even some 1950/60s examples. There are separate features on drovers' inns (p. 40), coaching inns (p. 88) and pubs that have other businesses run from them (p. 33).

Left: The Waterloo Hotel and Bistro Restaurant, Newport

Dathlu Treftadaeth Tafarnau Cymru

Llawlyfr ydyw *Real Heritage Pubs of Wales: Tafarnau Treftadaeth* i gasgliad hynod ac amrywiol o dafarnau gyda'r rhannau mewnol gorau a mwyaf diddorol yng Nghymru i gyd. Trwy hwn mae CAMRA yn achub y blaen wrth ddatblygu gwerthfawrogiad o du mewn tafarnau hanesyddol ymysg pobl lleol ac ymwelwyr fel ei gilydd. Er bod dros 4,000 o dafarnau yng Nghymru, dim ond tua 100 sydd yn y llawlyfr hwn. Mor ychydig ydynt o achos bod cymaint o agor i fyny, gosod themau a moderneiddio cyffredinol wedi digwydd yn y degawdau diwethaf. Mae diogelu beth sydd ar ol o dreftadaeth tafarnau ein gwlad wedi dod yn her ddifrifol yn nhermau cadwraeth. Wrth gyhoeddi y llawlyfr hwn, ein bwriad yw i annog perchnogion ac awdurdodau lleol i sicrhau bod y gemau hyn sydd wedi llwyddo i oroesi yn para fel tafarnau wirioneddol hanesyddol am flynyddoedd i ddod.

Mae'r llawlyfr yn adeiladu ar waith a ddechreuwyd gan CAMRA yn y 1990au cynnar i adnabod y tafarnau rheiny yn y Deyrnas Unedig gyda tu mewn hanesyddol yn dal mwy neu lai yn ei gyfanrwydd. Canlyniad hwn ydyw'r *National Inventory of Historic Pub Interiors* a cheir manylion o hwn ar www.heritagepubs.org.uk. Dim ond 11 o'r 288 dafarn ar y *National Inventory* cyfredol sydd yng Nghymru (adnabyddir hwy yn y llawlyfr hwn gan ★ neu ☆). I raddau helaeth mae'r tafarnau yn y llawlyfr hwn yn dal fel oeddent cyn canol y 1960au (pryd dechreuodd cyfnod trychinebus o ail-fampio tu mewn tafarnau ac agor ystafelloedd i fyny); neu, os ydynt wedi altro, mae hwn wedi digwydd mewn ffordd sensitif heb dinistrio calon hanesyddol y lle. Mae goroesiad mwy nac un ystafell, yn ogystal a hen ddodrefn a thaclau, wedi bod yn hanfodol wrth ddethol. Ceir wybodaeth pellach am waith CAMRA i achub dafarnau hanesyddol ar dudalen 28.

Mae'r llawlyfr hwn i dafarnau yng Nghymru hefo tu mewn hanesyddol yn cynnwys amrywiaeth eang o dafarnau i ymweld a nhw, eu hedmygu a'u mwynhau. Ar dudalennau 7–9 mae erthygl yn esbonio datblygiad y dafarn o dy cwrw syml ac yn datgelu'r llefydd lle gall rhywun yfed mewn man debyg iawn i ystafell flaen hen-ffasiwn! Mae'r erthygl ar arddull pensaerniol y dafarn Gymreig, ar dudalennau 94–5, yn crynhoi'r tafarnau a godwyd yn bwrpasol, o rai mawreddog oes Fictoria, trwy enghreifftiau o'r cyfnod rhwng rhyfeloedd, a hyd yn oed rhai o'r 1950au a'r 1960au. Ceir ysgrifau neilltuol ar dafarnau'r porthmyn (tud. 40), ar dafarnau'r goetsh fawr (tud. 88) ac ar dafarnau sydd a fusnesau eraill yn gysylltiedig a nhw (tud. 33).

How the Welsh Pub has Changed

Purpose-built inns reached Wales only in the last 300 years. This means that a number of the pubs featured in this guide are virtually indistinguishable from the thousands of farm houses and cottages scattered throughout the land. Often the only difference would have been a sign displaying the name and function of the building. The public drinking area would have been the main room or hall of the house, often around an inglenook fireplace.

This floor plan of the Red Lion, Llanegwad, shows how thousands of pubs operated in the past. The public room was the bar, being one of the domestic rooms allocated as such with no bar counter, just a fireplace. Beer is stored in the cellar, which is combined with the domestic pantry and is fetched from the cellar and served to your table. You have to go outside the building to the toilet. This plan also shows the remains of a malthouse as in the past some beer was produced on the premises.

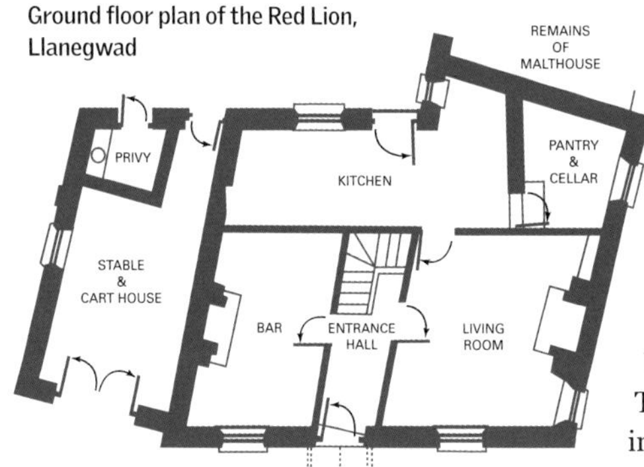

Ground floor plan of the Red Lion, Llanegwad

Beer Houses

The best of the few surviving examples of a 'beer house' in Wales today is the Goat, Llanfihangel-yng-Ngwynfa (p. 83), which is a rendered house in the middle of the village only distinguished by a pub sign on the side. The front door leads to the original main public room, which looks very domestic and small enough to appear like a hallway. Prior to the 1950s there were two other small rooms – the 'Bar bach' (small bar) situated to the rear left and another at the end of the passage but both of these are now in domestic use. In 1956 the family, who have been here for four generations, decided to convert the room on the right into the bar and installed a counter for the first time. The original main room is now used for 'overspill'.

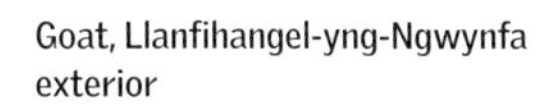
Goat, Llanfihangel-yng-Ngwynfa exterior

Dyffryn Arms, Pontfaen

Red Lion, Llansannan

The small lounge bar at the Grapes, Welshpool, has a 1950s tiled fireplace and the fixed seating is probably from that date.

Another rare surviving example of a beer house is the Dyffryn Arms, Pontfaen (p. 77), which has been in the same family ownership since it was built in 1845. Only the small sign board above the door makes it identifiable as a pub. Walk down the passage and left into what looks like an ordinary domestic room with the only difference being an opening with horizontally-sliding sashes to the ground floor cellar which is opened for service and closed afterwards.

The snug at the Red Lion, Llansannan (p. 45), is the outstanding example of settle seating arranged around the fireplace in what would have been the only public room in a domestic property with no bar counter, with beer fetched from the cellar to your table. Other excellent examples in Wales can be found at the Blue Bell, Llangurig (p. 87 and p. 88); the Mount Inn, Llanidloes (p. 86); and the Talbot, Tregaron (p. 39).

Terrace Pubs

Two pubs in this guide have developed from a beer house within a row of terraced houses. The Virginia Inn, Llanfairfechan (p. 44), originally consisted of the small rooms at the front left and rear right with a counter at the end of the passageway. Then the former domestic room at the front right was combined with the rear right one and another small room at the rear left was brought into pub use. At the Grapes, Welshpool (p. 89), the tiny public bar is unusually situated at the rear right and the other three rooms were brought into pub use over the years. The lounge bar at the front looks like it only came into public use in the 1950s when they cut a hatch into the wall for service to the back of the bar. Sadly, changes in 2007 saw the combination of the two rooms on the left.

Expansion of the Beer House

There are a number of pubs in this guide that remained as just one room with no bar counter and with beer fetched from the cellar until the 1950s/60s. Then they expanded, a bar counter was added and extra rooms opened as public rooms/bars. These include the Cross Inn,

This was the only room at the Rose & Crown, Graianrhyd until the early 1960s.

Glandy Cross (p. 32) in 1949; the Crown Inn, Llanfihangel Glyn Mwfyr (p. 44) in the 1950s; and the Sun, Rhewl (p. 50); Rose & Crown, Graianrhyd (p. 47); and New Inn, Llanddewi Brefi (p. 38) in the early 1960s.

Where to easily see the changes

At the *Good Beer Guide*-listed White Lion, Llanelian-yn-Rhos, Conwy, you can easily see how the interiors of Welsh pubs have changed over the years as there is a photo on the wall showing how it looked some 50 or so years ago. If you compare it to the layout today you will see it shows the inglenook fireplace is unchanged; the beer came from the cellar via a hatch (now the present servery i.e. a bar counter has been added); the settle is in a new position in the extension on the left; also the lounge to the rear was a later addition (in the late 1960s).

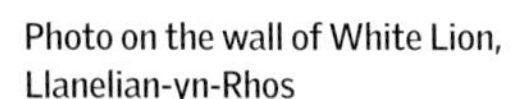
Photo on the wall of White Lion, Llanelian-yn-Rhos

There are examples of pubs in this guide where a hatch was replaced by a bar counter in recent years including the Prince of Wales, Cynwyd (p. 47), added in c.1960. The bar fittings of 1962 at the Colomendy Arms, Cadole (p. 50), probably replaced a hatch.

The left-hand door of the Globe, Maenclochog, Pembrokeshire, led into the village post office until the 1960s. The original pub was just the right-hand bar and the entrance door is on the right i.e. the one with the licensee details on it – this now leads to the domestic accommodation but some customers still use it. The 'new bar' on the left was opened for the investiture of Prince Charles as Prince of Wales in 1969 and a doorway-sized gap was created to link the two rooms.

Globe, Maenclochog

There are a number of pubs that were just one public bar with a counter until recent years when extra rooms/areas were added. At the Cresselly Arms, Cresswell Quay (p. 72), it is easy to spot the changes where the small single bar expanded into two former domestic rooms in 1981 – the domestic cooker is still there and in use. There is also a range fireplace at the Royal Hotel, Usk – see page 66 for a description of all the changes here.

Other pubs where expansions into parts of the property can be easily spotted include the New Cross, Court Henry (p. 30), where a former stable was converted into a dining room/lounge; the Old Point House, Angle (p. 71) where the one original room has been expanded to three; and the Carpenters Arms, Shirenewton (p. 64), which has expanded from one to seven rooms!

One of the former domestic rooms at the Carpenters Arms, Shirenewton.

Using this Guide

The main criterion for inclusion is the existence of a genuine historic setting in which to enjoy what people have enjoyed in pubs for centuries – a drink, good conversation and perhaps a bite to eat as well. It is not to be construed as a recommendation in any other sense. As with most pubs in Wales, you will be made welcome, especially if you say why you've taken the trouble to come and say a few complimentary words about the pub.

We have made considerable efforts to ensure the accuracy of the information at the time of going to press, but the licensed trade is currently experiencing unprecedented change so there will doubtless be changes occurring during the currency of this publication.

Accommodation

We have indicated the number of rooms available for let as well as indicating how many are en-suite. We have made no inspection of these parts of the pub and are not in a position to make any assessment of quality or price.

Food

Many users of this guide appreciate good food and the editors wish to point out that whilst quality food is available in many pubs in the book, searching it out is not our prime purpose and there are a number of other guides that are better placed to do it.

To be as helpful as possible, we have indicated where, at the time of going to press, a pub sells meals or snacks (at least toasted sandwiches or hot pies). If you are planning to visit a pub and require something to eat, we strongly recommend you ring in advance to check availability. Some pubs prefer you to make a booking, particularly for Friday and Saturday evenings, and kitchens can be closed at short notice, particularly if the licensee has changed or staff are not available.

Real ale

This indicates that the pub sells at least one cask-conditioned beer at the time of going to press. This is something that can change, and when you visit a pub without it on sale we encourage you to ask for real ale, as demand will result in more outlets. We also give an indication of which real ales you might expect to see on the bar – for more details see pages 58–9.

Real draught cider

We indicate if the pub sells at least one Welsh draught cider (or perry) or one from a producer in England.

Opening hours

Unless stated otherwise, the pubs are open at lunchtimes and evenings. We indicate where they are open all day; if they are closed on one particular session or day; and if the opening hours are different in summer and winter. 'Opens at 4pm' indicates the pub is closed lunchtimes, but opens from the stated time to evening closing time, usually 11pm.

A handful of pubs keep more restricted opening times and so we have tried to give an indication of these at the time of going to press. As opening hours can be subject to considerable change over time we strongly recommend you to phone ahead to check, particularly if you are travelling a long distance to a particular pub.

Key

★ A pub on Part One of CAMRA's *National Inventory of Historic Pub Interiors*, that is one that remains wholly or largely intact since before World War Two.

☆ A pub on Part Two of CAMRA's *National Inventory of Historic Pub Interiors*, that is one whose interior has been altered but which retains an exceptional room or feature of national historic importance.

🛏 Bed & Breakfast accommodation available.

⇌ Near railway station.

🚌 Bus routes that regularly pass close to the pub.

ISLE OF ANGLESEY/YNYS MÔN

Beaumaris/Biwmares
Castle Street LL58 8AP
01248 810329
www.bullsheadinn.co.uk
Grade II* listed
53/57/58 from Bangor
13 rooms and 13 in the Town House (all en-suite)
Meals lunchtimes and evenings in Brasserie (Loft Restaurant open evenings, not Sun.)
Real ales regularly including one Welsh

Ye Olde Bull's Head

The marvellous unspoilt public bar and a snug annexe to the left in this 17/18th century inn are barely altered in 50 years. This was a coaching inn on the London to Holyhead route prior to Telford's Menai Suspension Bridge. In the courtyard is what is recorded in *The Guinness Book of Records* as the largest simple-hinged door in Britain (11 feet wide and 13 feet high). The oldest pub fittings are the shelving at the rear of the servery in the public bar. As the photo from the 1960s on the wall above the fireplace shows there were large niches to the left and right of the fireplace but in recent years the left one has become an arched short passageway to link a former separate business. This is now a tiny snug bar, which has a brick bar counter of c.1960 with two old wooden hatch doors above and marble bar top. The entrance hall with a flagstone and tiled floor has an Art Nouveau decoration on a window to the bar/left side. The residents' lounge on the right was a shop in 1928. Open all day.

The last major changes to the public bar at Ye Olde Bulls Head, Beaumaris, were possibly around 1940, the date on the bank of three handpumps with red Bakelite handles. The brick fireplace, bar counter featuring four rows of 1930s-looking bricks and the red leather bay window seating could well date from c.1940. The stable door/hatch to the side looks much older.

Cemaes Bay
1 High Street LL67 0HH
01407 710205
Not listed
🚌 61 Holyhead–Amlwch, also 62 from Bangor evenings
Meals & snacks lunchtimes and evening

Old Vigour

The lounge bar is a classic example of how pubs were refitted in the 1960s, but very few of these interiors remain unchanged making this a rare survivor. The Old Vigour has been in the same family for 115 years and it remained little-altered until c.1960. The three existing small rooms were all refurbished and nothing much has changed since so this pub is stuck in a 1960s time warp. The oldest surviving fittings are the bar back shelves, best viewed from the small public bar. Also, note the old 'Commercial Room' wording on the door of the third room. The small smoke room at the front right, which is served from a hatch/doorway to the side of the bar, originally contained the hotel reception. Prior to the opening of the Catholic Church in 1965, church services were held in the lounge. Open all day.

At the Old Vigour, Cemaes Bay, a new bar was created in the 1960s in the former residents' lounge bar (a photo on the wall shows the original room) – this rare survivor remains totally unchanged.

Menai Bridge/ Porthaethwy
St. George's Pier, off Water Street LL59 5EY
01248 712453
www.liverpoolarms.info
Not listed
🚌 all buses from Bangor to Anglesey e.g. 4, 53, 57, 58, 62
Meals lunchtimes and also Wed. to Sat. evenings
Real ales

Liverpool Arms

Small multi-roomed mid-19th-century pub that has remained much as it was following a refit in the 1960s. The most characterful of its small rooms is the rear bar, which has a quarry-tiled floor, fixed seating from the 1960s and a small counter/hatch of similar age with a leatherette front. Above the old tongue-and-groove dado panelling in the public bar the walls are decorated with bric-a-brac including naval charts. A quarry-tiled hallway links the two small bars and to the right of it is the lounge, which until the 1960s comprised two rooms. Parking near the pub can be difficult but landlord Dave Menhennet suggests you use the pay & display car park behind Dafydd Hardy estate agents and when you pay for your round he will refund the parking fee! Open lunchtimes and evenings Mon. to Thu.; open all day Fri., Sat., & Sun.

The small public bar of the Liverpool Arms, Menai Bridge, has 1960s fixed seating and bar counter front, however the counter is possibly older and the bar back shelves on a mirrored back are considerably older.

TRY ALSO

The nearby **Victoria**, Telford Road LL59 5DR is a Georgian hotel with views overlooking the Menai Strait and is worth a visit for its lounge bar. Take the steps into the hotel and just past the reception hall is the wood-panelled bar with bar fittings dating from the 1960s. There is a public bar at the far left of the building with its separate entrance but the bar fittings only date from the mid-1980s. A sympathetic extension to the hotel was opened by cricketer Tony Lewis in 1998. Grade II listed; 01248 712309; www.vicmenai.com; Welsh real ale.

How Old is Old?

Many books about historic pubs and inns include details of 'the oldest pub in the country' but as a guide to real historic pub interiors we propose to take a different approach. Firstly, the dates we quote in this guide are properly researched, for example, in listing descriptions or the works of respected historians. There are all too many spurious and altogether hypothetical dates recycled in publications about pub 'heritage'.

We have tried to avoid dubious 'pub folklore' such as 'a secret tunnel to the church' – we have received a few such claims but no one has showed us any and most definitely no-one has provided an actual walk up one from end to end! This is also a 'ghost-free' guide (which, dull though it may be, is the probable true condition of most supposedly ghost-infested hostelries).

It is our view that what matters is the age of what we can see today – in terms of the building and, more importantly, the interior fixtures and fittings. It matters little for this guide if a building claims to be 13th century or is actually a 18th century rebuild if all the interior fittings date from 2008!

The vaulted undercroft of the **Llanthony Priory Hotel**, Llanthony

Earliest Recorded Inns

Llanthony Priory Hotel, Llanthony (p. 61) is part of a medieval structure making it the oldest building in this guide that is now a pub. In his excellent book *Historic Inns & Taverns of Wales & the Marches* (Stroud, 1993), Paul R Davis states there are very few genuine old inns. Most date from the 17th century or later and are linked to the improving road network from those times. Davis states that the Cross Keys, Swansea, 'could justly be claimed the oldest public house in Wales, since it was built around 1330 ... though it only became an inn at the end of the seventeenth century', the date of the frontage. It has a surviving 14th-century window at the rear and the building was renovated in the 1950s but is much extended and now has a modernised open-plan interior.

Pub Myth or Pub Fact?

Based on a claim of being mentioned as a pub in legal chronicles in 1110 (what these are is a mystery left to tease us), the Skirrid Mountain Inn, Llanfihangel Crucorney, states on its website that 'The Skirrid In... has stood for nine centuries'. However, the listing description of this Grade II building states that 'the present building appears wholly mid- to late-17th century with major alterations in the 19th century" – confirmed by John Newman in *The Buildings of Wales: Gwent/ Monmouthshire* (London, 2000). As the pub interior is much changed in recent years it did not meet the criteria for inclusion in this guide.

The Groes Inn, Ty'n-y-groes, in the Conwy valley claims the

'Wales's Oldest Inn' sign at the **Skirrid Mountain Inn**, Llanfihangel Crucorney

oldest license in Wales, dating from 1573 but the building is much extended and modernised.

Upstairs at the **Prince of Wales**, Kenfig, is the Kenfig Corporation Guildhall

Genuine History

The Prince of Wales, Kenfig (p. 16), which started life as Kenfig Corporation Guildhall and was built on pillars in the early 17th century, is an example of a genuinely old building featured in this guide. If you visit at a quiet time ask the landlord for a tour of 'the town hall' – the upstairs room with its 17th century wall-panelling; the wooden benches from its days as a court room; and the wall safe containing the mace that was presented to the ancient Borough of Kenfig in 1714 to celebrate the coronation of George I. Elsewhere, the Old Nag's Head, Monmouth (p. 62) incorporates a medieval round tower forming part of the old town walls, while the Blue Anchor, East Aberthaw (page 107), has been authoritatively dated to the mid-16th century (it claims 'Established c.1380'). This splendid thatched pub still retains a characterful interior of six rooms.

The **Blue Anchor**, East Aberthaw, a mid 16th century building, has a characterful interior of six rooms

BRIDGEND/PEN-Y-BONT AR OGWR

Kenfig/Cynffig
Maudlam CF33 4PR
01656 740356
Grade II listed
266 from Porthcawl
Meals Tue. to Sat. lunchtimes and evenings (not Mon., not Sun. evening)
Real ales including Welsh
Real Welsh draught cider

Prince of Wales/Ty Newydd

Originally the Kenfig Corporation Guildhall built on pillars in the early 17th century, the Prince of Wales was largely rebuilt in 1808. It was used as a court for many years and retains the judges' wooden benches, and some 17th-century wall panelling; part was used as a Sunday school room from 1864 to 2000. You can discover more about the pub's rich historic past by visiting www.kenfig.org.uk/history/prince-kenfig.html. The pub is still owned by the Kenfig Corporation Trust, which meets twice a year to distribute some £60,000 (the rents from this and other properties) to local groups and organisations who apply for grants. Downstairs the pub still retains three rooms. To the left of the passage with an old Worthington mirror on the wall there is a small room with panelling and a fireplace from the 1970s. Beyond this is the small 'Singing Room' with old seating and a hatch to the side of the bar. In the middle of the pub lies the servery and beyond that you can see the casks on stillage in the cellar, which was extended back in recent years. The counter was replaced in the 1970s when they removed a tiny area to the right known as the 'Royal Box' (floor markings indicate its position) used by select customers who would serve themselves. The large room in front of the servery was formerly three small rooms and a passageway, but has been like this for at least 40 years. The Prince of Wales is run on traditional lines with no jukebox, no fruit machines, no pool table and the TV is only switched on for rugby. Open all day.

The small left hand room of the Prince of Wales, Kenfig.

CAERPHILLY/CAERFFILI

Gilfach Fargoed
Park Place CF81 8LW
01443 830272
Not listed
Gilfach Fargoed
50 Newport–Bargoed, X38 Pontypridd–Bargoed
3 rooms (all en-suite)
Meals lunchtimes (not Sun.); evening meals by request.
Real ales including one Welsh
Real Welsh draught cider

Capel

This traditional local built in 1912 of red brick is a rare example of a little-altered multi-room pub. Built by Philips Brewery of Newport it is named after John Capel Hanbury, a local landowner. The original layout remains apart from the amalgamation of the Jug & Bottle with the public bar by the removal of a partition, however, the etched glass panel in the door remains. The large public bar retains its original solid carved counter and splendid mirrored bar-back with a still-working dumb waiter. Several windows survive recording varied room names including Commercial Room, which has a hatch/bar to the rear with intact sash windows; and Buffet Bar, which has good fixed seating but a modern counter. Beyond a partition wall on the far left is a terrazzo floor passage – note the ornate brass door handles. There is a non-working gas light in the public bar. Skittles is played in an upstairs room. Open all day.

Right: The magnificent old weighing machine in the left hand passage of the Capel, Gilfach Fargoed, originally came from a railway station and has in the past been used to weigh prize-fighters.

The public bar of the Capel, Gilfach Fargoed, where the counter was shortened by some 7 feet on the left to enable access to the rear room.

Machen
Nant-y-Ceisiad (100 yards north of A468 at west end of village)
CF83 8QQ
01633 441005
www.whitehartinn.org.uk
Not listed
50 from Newport
4 rooms
Meals lunchtimes (not Wed.) and evenings
Real ales including Welsh

On the ceiling in the main bar of the White Hart, Machen, is a large oval shaped painting that has suffered from nicotine staining – you can see what it should look like on the photo situated in the alcove on the way to the kitchen.

White Hart

And now for something completely different! As you walk into the White Hart you may get the feeling that you are walking on board a passenger liner, and in a way you are. The pub is fitted out with panelling, many pieces of furniture and a marble fireplace from the 1947 refurbishment of the first class liner *SS Empress* of France (built as *SS Duchess of Bedford* in 1928), from the breakers John Cashmore of Newport. This thorough refit took place in 1961, when the entrance was moved from one end to the other and the pub was extended front and back, and this most unusual pub has barely changed since. At the rear is a lounge/function room with a 'sunken' bar, brass bar top and ply panelled walls. The pub very occasionally brews its own beers. Open lunchtimes (not Wed.) and evenings.

Corks: a Pub Game in the South Wales Valleys

A game of corks, at the **Fox and Hounds**, Risca, Caerphilly, which is played on Sunday lunchtimes from September to March.

Corks is a pub game played only in Wales and not in any other part of the UK. Based on a game seen played with metal weights in North Wales some 50 years ago that may have originated in France, nowadays it can be seen in the South Wales valleys where there are two leagues. One was set up around Abercarn and Crumlin in 1956 and the Ynysddu League, founded in 1959, takes in teams from Risca, Crosskeys, Pontywaun and Cwmfelinfach. There are about fourteen pub and club teams in each league, but it never seems to have spread any further.

The game is played on a long piece of chipboard, hinged in three pieces and unfolded flat exactly over the dartboard mat. Five corks, painted white and numbered 1 to 5, are placed on a circle. You throw three corks, painted black, underhand, one at a time, trying to knock the white corks out of the circle. Like all simple looking games, corks is harder than it looks. For a start, there is an irresistible temptation to put one foot along side the board, to gain half a yard advantage. The locals will soon put you right on this: "Getting our feet a bit wet, then, are we? Fish biting?" – a polite way of saying "get both feet behind the throwing line or else"!

Pentwyn
Ogilvie Road CF81 9NP
01685 841215
Not listed
1 Merthyr Tydfil–Bargoed
Meals lunchtimes and evenings

White Horse

One of the highest pubs in Wales, situated 1300ft above sea level between the Taff and Rhymney valleys, this three-roomed pub was built in 1860. The star here is the public bar on right, which retains its Victorian curved counter and bar back with a row of what looks like old haberdashery shop style drawers. The last changes were in the 1960s when the original door into the bar was blocked up and the entrance moved to the present one. The lounge on the left up a few steps was refurbished in the 1960s and is served from a stable door hatch to the old bar. At the rear of the bar is a bare boarded games room with 1960s panelled walls and a brick fireplace from the 1950s. The room is served by a split door hatch to the back of the bar and has a 1960s Artex ceiling.

Below: The old range fireplace at the White Horse, Pentwyn, and some fixed bench seating which was apparently salvaged from a local church, possibly in the 1960s.

Right: The Victorian bar fittings of the White Horse, Pentwyn – one of the sections of the bar back does not have a counter in front of it because it was slightly shortened on the left in the 1960s.

TRY ALSO

The only pub we have found in Merthyr Tydfil county that has a historic pub interior is the **Cardigan Arms**, Victoria Street, Dowlais CF48 3RW. In a terrace of shops and houses, this is a drinkers' pub still retaining three small rooms. A passage runs from the front door to the rear and has some old dado panelling and a hatch to the side of the bar. The small public bar on the right has an old bar counter but this has a frontage added in 2005; fixed seating dates from the 1960s. On the left is the lounge with ply panelling attached to the walls and more 1960s fixed seating. At the rear is the games room, served from a hatch to the rear of the servery.

CARDIFF/CAERDYDD

Adamsdown
200 Broadway, corner of Beresford Road CF24 1QJ
029 2047 3984
www.theroyaloakcardiff.co.uk
Grade II listed
30, 44, 45, 49/50
5 rooms
Meals lunchtimes Fri., Sat. & Sun and also early evening Fri., Sat. & Sun.
Brains real ales

Royal Oak

Late 19th century pub that has still retained its four rooms and an excellent set of four stained glass window screens along the Beresford Road frontage. There is more stained glass in the panels between the servery and the snug; both rear snugs retain their original tiled fireplaces. The lounge on the far left which doubles as a function room has modern bar fittings but the fixed seating is old. For many years the Royal Oak was run by the relatives of featherweight champion "Peerless" Jim Driscoll, including Kitty Flynn who lived here from 1946 to 2003, which may explain why the interior is little-altered. The pub still sports many boxing mementos and above the lounge was Driscoll's Boxing Gym (which closed in 2006, but may reopen). There is a live band every Fri. and Sat. evening, also a Jam night on Wed. Open all day.

The fine bar back with mirror strips and painted glass panels in the public bar of the Royal Oak, Cardiff; the counter is a post war replacement.

Some of the plaster relief figures on the wall of one snug at the Royal Oak, Cardiff.

The nearby **Cardiff Arms**, 63 Railway Street, Splott CF24 2DF is an 1890s built three-storey pub that retains two small rooms on the left hand with fittings from the 1950s, but they are only open in order to gain access to the smoking area at the rear. Brains real ale.

Preserving Historic Pub Features

This fine set of four window screens at the **Royal Oak**, Adamsdown, Cardiff now restored and on show in the public bar.

CAMRA applauds careful conservation of historic pub features. If a pub is listed there is a statutory requirement to keep historic fabric in order and if damaged it should be accurately replaced. There are two Cardiff pubs where window glass has been damaged in recent years and the owners, in both cases it was Brains Brewery, have spent money on replacement or refurbishment. The set of four window screens at the Royal Oak, Adamsdown Cardiff had suffered damage over the years and in 2008 Brains carried out a superb restoration.

Exterior windows are the most vulnerable historic fittings and at the Old Arcade, Cardiff the window with the rare 'Luncheon Bar' wording was smashed a few years ago.

While Brains are to be commended for arranging the replacement glass with the Luncheon Bar wording, sadly, it is a poor replica of the original one.

TRY ALSO In Roath the **Claude Hotel**, 140 Albany Road CF24 3RW is well worth a visit to see the comfortable panelled Oak Room on the left hand side. The pub was built in 1890 and was refitted in the 1930s. The Oak Room is typical of the better rooms in large town pubs of the inter-war years and even though the pub had a refurbishment in 2005 the locals insisted that no changes were made to it! The Oak Room was a men-only lounge up to the early 1970s – the Sex Discrimination Act came into force on 1 January 1976. The public bar is a large modern room created in 1994 by the amalgamation of the public bar, a ladies snug and a skittle alley at the rear. 029 2049 3896; Real ale.

TRY ALSO In Llandaff the **Butchers Arms**, High Street, CF5 2DZ, near the cathedral, retains a virtually untouched small public bar with Victorian bar counter and bar back. The smoke room on the right opens up to the room behind where the counter could be 40 years old; and through an arch is another small room. 029 2055 1000; Real ales including guest ones.

Cathays
29 Gwennyth Street CF24 4PH
029 2039 8020
Not listed
28
No food
Brains real ales

Gower

Built in 1898 of orange-red brick, this huge pub in a residential area still retains its multi-roomed interior including an intact billiards room. This back street community local has windows with good 20th century glass with the name of the brewery – Brain's – and Gower Hotel. The public bar on the left has dado panelling, fixed seating and counter that could all date from c.1960. A wide doorway on the left of the bar leads to the small smoke room, now the pool room, with an old Brain's mirror and c.1960 dado panelling. The blocked-up exterior door between the bar and the lounge was the former off-sales, now a kitchen. The lounge with its separate entrance on the right has a c.1960 ply dado in the hallway and in the two-part lounge itself, which was two small rooms in the past. This is the venue for a Sunday afternoon folk jam session. The bar fittings are modern but the gents' has two old urinals. There is a skittle alley to the rear left and also a long narrow function room upstairs which hosts a music club every 1st Thu. (and possibly 3rd Thu.) of the month and has a bar added c.1960 in a side room. In the garden is the clocking-on point for the local pigeon fanciers club. Open all day.

Left: The public bar of the Gower, Cardiff, retains its original Victorian bar back fitting with slender columns and capitals.

Snooker Plus/Billiard Tables in Pubs in Wales

The high ceilinged billiards room at the **Gower**, Cardiff has an interesting roof with the arch-braces to the beams. It retains a full-sized snooker table – the makers label states 'The New Improved Express Match Cushions Billiard Table, Robert Graham & Sons Ltd., Grosvenor Billiard Works, Cardiff, Est. 1921'.

There are three pubs in this book that have a full-sized Snooker Table still in use – the Castle, Barry (p. 105), the Douglas Arms, Bethesda (p. 53); and the Gower, Cathays, Cardiff (p. 22). Also, there is one upstairs at the Ty Brith, Carno (p. 80) but it is currently disused, and one was removed from the rear room of the Oak Tree, Wrexham (p. 111) in recent years.

On the full-sized table at the Douglas Arms, Bethesda, they play the rare game of Snooker Plus. It was invented by Joe Davis in 1959 and includes two extra balls – an orange (scores 8) and a purple (scores 10). This means the possible maximum break is 210, something not even 15-times World Champion Joe could score! (but it is believed to have been achieved by Jimmy White, date unknown).

The Billiard Table at the **Douglas Arms**, Bethesda, set up for the game of Snooker Plus has a purple ball between the brown and blue, and an orange ball between the blue and pink.

Cardiff City Centre/ Canol Dinas Caerdydd

282–283 Bute Street, corner of Customhouse Street CF10 1GH
029 2034 3129
www.thegoldencrosscardiff.com
Grade II listed
Cardiff Central
all serving city centre
Meals until 8pm
Brains real ales

Golden Cross ☆

The Golden Cross has the most spectacular pub interior in the whole of Wales. Built in 1903 with excellent S A Brain & Co. Ltd. lettering on its colourful faience exterior, which gives you an indication of what to expect inside. In 1978 it was under threat of demolition for road widening but a campaign saved it and then Brains carried out a restoration, reopening the pub in 1986. On entering you will see some spectacular Craven Dunnill decorative tilework on the walls of the main public bar in various shades of brown and green on the dado and yellow and green above, topped off with a colourful floral pattern frieze above. The tiles also run up the side of the open staircase. There also two hand-painted pictorial panels completed by Craven Dunnill of Jackfield, Shropshire for the opening of the pub in 1903. The large one in the public bar is of Cardiff Castle – see page 25. In the left-hand room is one of the Old Town Hall in 1863. (There is also a tile panel of Brains Old Brewery in St Mary Street, Cardiff at around 1890 in the left hand lobby but this dates from c.1980). The impressive original bar backs remain in the main bar and in the lounge on the right, but the counter in the latter is modern. There has been some opening-up to the rear of the main bar and this area, which is popular with diners, has modern fittings. The pub has a good set of Brain's leaded windows. Please note that this is Cardiff city centre's premier gay pub in the evenings with live music late Sun. and late Wed. Open all day until 2am (3am Sat.).

One of the two tiled paintings at the Golden Cross, Cardiff.

Top right: The colourful faience exterior of the Goldon Cross, Cardiff, gives you a foretaste of what to expect inside.

The long L-shaped counter of the Golden Cross, Cardiff – one of only 20 remaining ceramic bar counters left in the whole of the UK – which features grotesques on the frontage. There is another equally impressive counter in Wales at the Waterloo, Newport (p. 69).

Protecting Historic Pub Interiors

With so few unspoilt pub interiors in Wales, it is critically important to preserve what survives. Yet only 47 per cent of the pubs in this guide are statutorily 'listed' by Cadw, the heritage arm of the Welsh Assembly Government (WAG).

Buildings are listed because of their special architectural or historic interest, or their value as a group. Importantly, listing relates to both the exterior and the interior of a building with three classifications:

Grade I – Buildings of exceptional, usually national, interest. (Under two per cent of buildings listed in Wales qualify);

Grade II* – Particularly important buildings of more than special interest;

Grade II – Buildings of special interest, which warrant every effort being made to preserve them.

Llanthony Priory Hotel, Llanthony (p. 61) is a Grade I listed building for its medieval origi

The 'Listed Building Consent' Process

Cadw compiles the lists of buildings and in considering whether to list a building local authorities and the Royal Commission on the Ancient and Historical Monuments of Wales (RCAHMW) are also consulted.

Local planning authorities are then responsible for operating the system through listed building consent. The need for consent applies to all parts of the building, interior or exterior, regardless of grade and whether or not the feature is mentioned in the official list description. The local planning authority examines the application against national guidelines issued by WAG and its policies for the protection of the historic environment. In addition there will be a presumption in favour of preservation.

This process offers listed buildings protection from damaging change. However, only one of the pubs featured in this guide is Grade I listed; there are three Grade II* listed pubs; and a further 40 are Grade II listed. This means over half of the real heritage pubs of Wales are unlisted.

Many of Wales's statutorily listed pubs do not appear in this guide as they are listed for reasons other than their interiors, e.g. a fine external appearance; or their interiors have been too altered. Until recently pub interiors received little attention from mainstream planning and conservation bodies.

The hall of **Ye Old Bull's Head**, a Georgian hotel in Beaumaris (p. 11), one of only three pubs included in this guide that are Grade II* listed (the others are the Blue Anchor, East Aberthaw (p. 107) and Old Nags Head, Monmouth (p. 62)).

Historic Pub Interiors at Risk

Recent experience indicates that many of the interiors of pubs in this guide that lack listed building status are at risk from damaging changes. Action is therefore required. The only way that proposed changes can undergo proper scrutiny by the local community is for the pub to be statutorily listed, so that applications for changes have to be made to the local authority and a statutory period of consultation allowed.

The tiled painting of Cardiff Castle is one of the stunning interior features of the **Golden Cross**, Cardiff (p. 23), but this pub is only a Grade II listed building and the listing description does not emphasise the rarity of the interior features.

Helping to Save Historic Pub Interiors in Wales

CAMRA believes that all the pubs included in this book are worthy of protection and sensitive treatment.

CAMRA is already working with Cadw with a view to encouraging them to statutorily list more of the pubs in this guide and will be requesting them to include the appropriate reference to the rarity of layouts/interior fittings in listed descriptions.

CAMRA will be writing to all local planning authorities to point out how few pubs with historic interiors remain asking for their help to protect them for future generations. Also, where a pub does not qualify for statutory listing we will be asking them to add the pubs to a 'local list' of historic buildings.

The **Halfway House**, Llanelli (p.35) has some of the finest Victorian bar fittings in Wales but the pub is not currently protected by statutory listing.

Included on Cardiff City Council's 'local list' is **Claude**, Roath, Cardiff (p. 21) whose little changed Oak Room retains its fireplace, fixed seating and wall panelling with bell pushes from the 1930s.

TRY ALSO

In Cardiff there are two other notable ceramic pub frontages – the **Queens Vaults**, 29 Westgate Street CF10 1DA has a bright yellow one including elaborate lettering of 'Queens Vaults', 'Wines', 'Ind Coope & Co. Ltd. Entire', ('Entire' being a beer better known as porter.) Also, the **Vulcan**, 10 Adam Street CF24 2FH, has a lovely brown and green glazed ceramic frontage with a fascia 'The Vulcan', 'Wines & Spirits' 'Hotel', 'Ales & Stouts'. The Vulcan dating from 1853 was sadly changed in the 1970s when a partition was removed from the public bar, which has a new bar counter and bar back. A passage down the right hand side leads to a small lounge to the rear with a splendid ornate ceramic fireplace. Don't miss the gents' toilets outside with its three massive very old brown urinals! 029 2046 1580; Brains real ale.

Cardiff City Centre/ Canol Dinas Caerdydd
14 Church Street CF10 1BG
029 2021 7999
www.sabrain.com/oldarcade
Not listed
Cardiff Central
all serving city centre
Meals until 6pm (4.30pm Sun.)
Brains real ales and occasional guest beer

Old Arcade

The Old Arcade is one of the most famous rugby pubs in the world – it is well worth a visit to see a contrast of fittings with early 20th century ones in the front bar and some genuine late-Victorian fittings in the back bar. It is very busy when there is an event at the nearby Millennium Stadium, particularly rugby matches. It was built in 1844 as the Birdcage Inn; and later called the Arcade Vaults. In the front bar the counter looks like inter-war work, as does the wall panelling and there is a 1920s style fireplace. There are several doors into the front bar indicating it was probably sub-divided in the past. The remaining bar back is in a neo-Jacobean style – note the little upright barrels in the decoration – it has been altered to incorporate a genuine Victorian mirror that was formerly on the wall of the lounge. Note the original 'Brains Beer' etched window. Later refurbishments give the pub a modern feel but it is good to see a city centre pub retaining many old fittings. Open all day.

The back bar of the Old Arcade, Cardiff, retains this splendid late Victorian bar back fitting still with five of the six original mirrored panels; also a mahogany counter and an early 20th century fireplace.

Changes made to the front bar of the Old Arcade, Cardiff in 1995 included the shortening of the bar counter, removing it from the front of the room so you are now only served from the side. Note part of the old bar back fitting at the front still remains.

TRY ALSO

Just north of Cardiff in the village of Pentyrch the **Kings Arms**, Church Road CF15 9QF is worth a visit to see the small flagstone floor bar with large early 18th century stone fireplace, with a bake oven and an ancient high backed settle. It has barely changed in the past 50 years when the small curved bar counter was added. There are large bars to the left and right but these have modern fittings. Grade II listed; 029 2089 0202; www.sabrain.com/kings-arms; Brains real ale and occasional guest beer.

CARMARTHENSHIRE/SIR GÂR

Carmarthen/Caerfyrddin
St. Mary's Street SA31 1TN
01267 222151
Grade II listed
🚌 all serving town centre
⇌ Carmarthen
No food

Plume of Feathers

Possibly the smallest pub in Wales, yet it still has two separate rooms. A famous rugby pub, it has lots of memorabilia on the walls including signed photos by international players such as Ray Gravell. On the side of the three-storey mid-19th-century building it is recorded that a team sponsored by the pub won the World Tournament Rugby Sevens in 1989 held at Amsterdam. Note the trap door in the floor, which is how the beer is dropped into the cellar. Between the two rooms are staircases – down to the toilets and up to private quarters. A number of famous actors including Richard Harris, Oliver Reed, and Richard Burton drank in the pub while filming 'Under Milk Wood' in nearby Laugharne. Open all day from 9/10am and may close early weekday evenings.

The Plume of Feathers, Carmarthen, has a tiny bar on the left with a slatted wood counter at least 30 years old, simple shelves for a bar back, which look older, dado panelled walls with benches attached, and a hatch on the right. An even tinier lounge on the right has some old panelling around the fireplace but the fixed seating is post-war.

Saving the UK's Pub Heritage

Real Heritage Pubs of Wales and other similar guides have grown out of CAMRA's concern about the rapid disappearance of our pub heritage and the major survey it initiated in the early 1990s to identify and campaign for the survival of the best remaining examples. The main aim was to list those interiors that remained very much as they had been before the Second World War and/or still had features of exceptional historic or architectural importance.

After six years' work, CAMRA's first *National Inventory of Pub Interiors of Outstanding Historic Interest* (now called 'National Inventory of Historic Pub Interiors') appeared – there was a total of just 179 pubs, including 5 in Wales, such had been the scale of modern change. Visit CAMRA's Heritage Pubs website, www.heritagepubs.org.uk, for an up-to-date list with full descriptions plus photographs.

The *National Inventory of Historic Pub Interiors* comes in two parts: Part One consists of historic interiors which are listed for their intactness while Part Two contains ones which, although altered, still retain features or rooms of truly national significance.

CAMRA has already produced Regional Inventories of Historic Pub Interiors for Greater London, East Anglia, and North East England; also one for Scotland and this guide for Wales. Guides for Yorkshire and the East Midlands are in preparation and ones for other regions will follow soon. Details of Northern Ireland's Real Heritage Pubs are available on www.heritagepubs.org.uk

The **Golden Cross**, Cardiff (p. 23), is on CAMRA's *National Inventory of Historic Pub Interiors* Part Two for its spectacular tiled interior.

The **Fox**, Ysceifiog (p. 52), is on CAMRA's *National Inventory of Historic Pub Interiors* Part One for its four-room interior, intact since the 1930s

Protection for More Pubs

In the mid 1990s English Heritage jointly funded with CAMRA a project to statutorily list many pubs and improve the listing description of many more so that the features of their historic interior were highlighted. Following the launch of *Scotland's True Heritage Pubs*, Historic Scotland carried out a Thematic Review of Public Houses which resulted in the statutory listing of more pubs, raising the grade of a number and expanding the listing descriptions of many more. CAMRA is already working with Cadw with a view to encouraging them to statutorily list more of the pubs in this guide.

The **Lion Royal Hotel**, Rhayader (p. 90), is a pub on CAMRA's *National Inventory of Historic Pub Interiors* Part Two for its unchanged small public bar of 1921.

Conservation and Commercial Operations

It is a major aim of these guides to get genuine historic pub interiors visited and appreciated. As each guide is produced, CAMRA makes a point of drawing the pubs included in them to the attention of planning departments of the local authorities in which they lie. We believe that with a combination of awareness by the public and pub owners on one hand and local authority vigilance on the other, the pubs listed should have a bright and long-lived future without damaging change.

Pubs, of course, are commercial businesses and have been constantly changing through time but it does seem sensible both in terms of conserving our heritage and as a matter of good business sense to look after the relatively few genuine old interiors we have left. There are examples amongst other building types such as religious and railway buildings where heritage is seen as an opportunity rather than a drawback and we encourage the owners of real heritage pubs to promote them as such.

If a pub is not included in this guide that does not mean it is devoid of historic value.

The **Crown & Anchor**, Llanidloes (p. 85), is a pub on CAMRA's *National Inventory of Historic Pub Interiors* Part One for its rare multi-roomed interior.

We have had to draw the line somewhere, so you will still come across pubs with features like etched glass, old bar fittings and tile-work that are a joy to behold and deserve to be saved.

How You Can Help

Do you know of other pubs to include? With so many pubs across such a vast area, there may be historic examples that have escaped our notice – if you find one, do please let us know. *Real Heritage Pubs of Wales*, like the *National Inventory of Historic Pub Interiors*, is an organic document to be kept under constant review and updated in the light of feedback and further research. If you have any updates, comments or suggestions for pubs to include in future editions, please email us at info.pubheritage@camra.org.uk or write to Pub Heritage Group, CAMRA, 230 Hatfield Road, St Albans AL1 4LW.

Carmarthen/Caerfyrddin
Queen Street SA31 1JR
01267 231800
Grade II listed
Carmarthen
all serving town centre
No accommodation
Meals 10am to 6pm
Real ales including Welsh

Queens Hotel

A three-storey hotel rebuilt in 1865, it retains a three-room layout last refitted in the late 1950s. The bar counter with its Formica top looks like it is from that era and both rooms have 1950s brick fireplaces. The bar on the right has another brick fireplace from the 1950s and a brick bar, which is more modern. There is a hatch to the back of the bar at the head of the passage that leads to the toilets at the rear. The licensee owns Hamilton's Restaurant next door. Open all day.

On the left side of the Queens Hotel, Carmarthen, are two small panelled rooms separated by a wooden folding partition, which nowadays is kept permanently open.

Court Henry/Cwrt Henri
1 mile north of the A40
SA32 8SD
01558 668276
Not listed
Meals Sat. evenings & Sun. lunchtimes

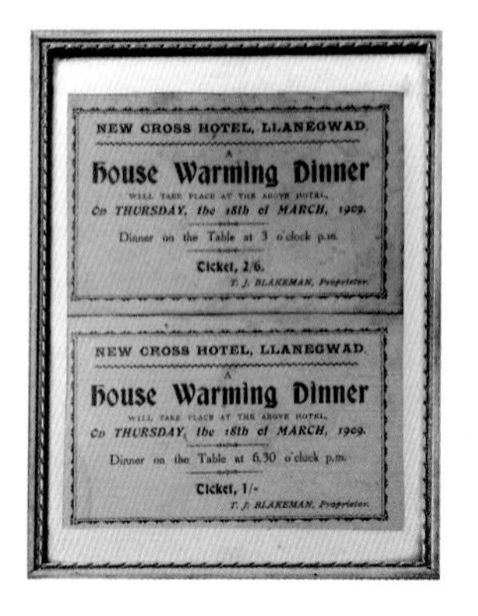

NEW CROSS HOTEL, LLANEGWAD.
A
House Warming Dinner
WILL TAKE PLACE AT THE ABOVE HOTEL,
On THURSDAY, the 18th of MARCH, 1909.
Dinner on the Table at 3 o'clock p.m.
Ticket, 2/6.
T. J. BLAKEMAN, Proprietor.

NEW CROSS HOTEL, LLANEGWAD.
A
House Warming Dinner
WILL TAKE PLACE AT THE ABOVE HOTEL,
On THURSDAY, the 18th of MARCH, 1909.
Dinner on the Table at 6.30 o'clock p.m.
Ticket, 1/-
T. J. BLAKEMAN, Proprietor.

New Cross ☆

This pub is a truly remarkable survival – still part of a 200-acre livestock farm, it celebrated its 100th birthday in 2009 and the public bar has survived virtually without change. In the past it was quite common for pub-keeping to be combined with some other livelihood but it is rare these days. Another remarkable fact about the New Cross, Court Henry, is that we know to the day when it opened – 18 March 1909 – as invitations to the opening dinner are preserved in a frame on the mantleshelf. The 100th birthday celebrations lasted three days and the pub was featured on TV. The small public bar with its red and black quarry-tile floor retains a matchboarded counter, simple shelving behind and a wooden fire-surround, complete with shelving and small turned balusters and a 'Truman, Hanbury & Buxton & Co Burton Ales' mirror above. The only modern item is some leatherette fixed seating from the late 1960s. Note the old opener on the counter that was used for taking corks out of beer bottles. When built the pub consisted of the public bar and also a smoking room – note a door on the left of the porch – but this other small room became part of the living quarters in the 1960s. At this time the old stables to the right were converted into a large restaurant/new lounge that can hold 100 diners. Accessed through a

The public bar of the New Cross, Court Henry is virtually the same as it was when it opened in 1909.

pair of doors on the right of the bar with a small hatch to the side of the bar for service and ply panelled walls it impacts little on the old bar. It is used for meals on a Saturday evening and also one sitting at 12.30pm for an amazingly good value three-course Sunday roast lunch for which a booking is essential. Opening hours are limited to most Thursday evenings (i.e. best to ring to check), every Sat. evening from 7pm, and Sun. lunchtimes from 12 to 3pm.

Cwmdu, near Llandeilo
Talley Road SA19 7DY
01558 685088 (pub & shop)
www.cwmdu.com
Grade II listed
Self catering in three cottages in the terrace (0844 8002070/www.nationaltrustcottages.co.uk)
Meals: Sat. evenings (booking recommended)
Welsh real ale
Real draught cider

Cwmdu Inn

The Cwmdu Inn and its separate small shop have been run by the villagers since 2000. A visit is highly recommended to see both, particularly the small public bar where you will soon be drawn into conversation accompanied by good beer – the essence of a traditional pub. It is part of an early 19th century terrace including a small shop/post office and holiday cottages and has been owned by the National Trust since 1991. Both the pub and shop were in the hands of Miss Annie Griffiths for 50 years until she died in 1987 aged 98. Since 2000 it has been run by a volunteer community structure in a unique partnership with the National Trust. Cymdeithas Cwmdu holds monthly meetings to run the pub and shop; also events such as Cwmdu Fete last Sat. in June; Apple Day 1st Sat. (possibly 2nd) in October etc. On 23rd October 2009

On the left of the Cwmdu Inn, Cwmdu, is the public bar with the figure '1' on the door and behind it the original servery. This very small public bar was Annie Griffiths' living room and as part of the restoration in 1994 the National Trust added a small counter/hatch by cutting a hole in the wall on the servery side.

A flagstone corridor runs from the front door of the Cwmdu Inn, Cwmdu, to the servery at the rear with a figure '2' on the door. On the right is the original public room, as there was no bar in Annie's day, and the beer was fetched from the servery.

HRH Prince Charles, Prince of Wales and President of the National Trust visited Cwmdu including its inn and shop and the locals will keenly show you photos from the event. The room on the right has a flagstone floor, large stone fireplace with a log fire, old settle and a dartboard. It acts as the restaurant room on a Sat. (beyond it is a kitchen), and is used for quiz nights; folk evenings 1st Fri. of month; Classic Club every 2nd Thu. of month; if rugby is on TV; and if the public bar is full. The tiny bar has a flagstone floor, two settles and just a couple of tables. The beer is from Evan Evans brewed in nearby Llandeilo, usually the 4.0% Cwrw (Welsh for beer). There are small rooms upstairs, which are brought into use as required for example if there are a lot of people dining on a Sat. night. The pub is open Wed. to Sat. 7pm to 11pm.

Glandy Cross

North of Efailwen on A478 SA66 7XB

01994 419280

Not listed

No food (Café Beca is ¾ mile south on the A478)

430 Cardigan–Narberth, three journeys each way per day

Cross Inn

A small locals' pub little changed since c.1950. Prior to that the only bar was the room on the right and it was served via a hatch. The red quarry-tiled floor, however, is much older and probably dates back to the Victorian days of the pub. The brick fireplace dates from c.1950 and one section of the 1950s seating remains. Across the quarry-tiled passage from front door to rear is a lounge/pool room, the front part has more c.1950 hardboard fixed seating and at the rear a 1950s brick fireplace. The rear section was originally the private sitting room. At the end of the passage is a tiny but popular lino tiled snug with just one table. Open all day.

In the 1950s a hatch was changed to an arch over a lapped wood counter in the public bar of the Cross Inn, Glandy Cross, and bar back shelves added to ply-panelled walls.

'A Pint of Bitter and Half a Dozen Eggs Please'

Almost without exception, pubs are now stand-alone businesses but this has not always been the case. Here we give examples of combined trades that were in existence in the past and some examples of where this still continues today.

Shops Past and Present

In the tiny village of Cwmdu, near Llandeilo there is a most impressive survivor. Situated in an early 19th-century terrace, the Cwmdu Inn (p. 31) and its separate small shop & post office have been run by the villagers since 2000. The shop and post office is open Tue. to Fri. 9.30am to 1pm; and Sat. 9.30am to 12.30pm.

Until 1960 the Cross, Hayscastle Cross, Pembrokeshire included a shop and Post Office and although they no longer exist the pub still sells newspapers and eggs.

The **Cwmdu Inn**, Cwmdu (p. 31), and its separate small shop and post office.

The present public bar at the front right of the Crown & Anchor, Llanidloes (p. 85), was brought into use c.1948, having previously been a haberdashery shop. Other pubs in this guide that once included another business include the Royal Hotel, Usk (p. 66) where behind the front right hand shop window there was originally an undertakers. The Carpenters Arms, Shirenewton (p. 64) is so named as it was previously also a carpentry business.

The No Sign Bar, Swansea (p. 102), was Munday's wine merchants shop with bars behind. These glazed cabinets are probably those used to display the wares on offer.

The main bar of the **Crown & Anchor**, Llanidloes (p. 85) – previously a haberdashery shop

The former wine merchants shop part of the **No Sign Bar**, Swansea (p. 102).

The Farmer Publican

Colin Blakeman is a farmer by day and here landlord in his tiny public bar at the New Cross, Court Henry (p. 30) which opens most Thursday evenings, every Saturday evening and Sunday lunchtimes. This amazing survivor is still part of a 200-acre livestock farm. The Dyffryn Arms ('Bessie's'), Pontfaen (p. 77) is still linked to a small-holding with ten acres of farmland plus six of woodland.

The **New Cross**, Court Henry (p. 30), public bar with farmer landlord Colin Blakeman.

Llandovery/Llanymddyfri
2 Market Square SA20 0AA
01550 720813
Grade II listed
Llandovery
280/281 from Carmarthen, 299 from Brecon
No food
Real ale

Red Lion ★

This is a unique no-frills market-town time warp pub – one of only two in Wales without a bar counter. The building itself is 18th and 19th century and part may be older still. It has a two-storey, symmetrical front to the market square and has the attractive feature of a pentice roof supported on iron columns running the whole length of the building and sheltering the ground floor. The front door leads to a red quarry-tiled passage and just past the inner doors the bar is a small room on the right with an alcove at the front called 'the lounge' which is filled with bric-a-brac. There is a small hatch and a door leading to the cellar servery at the rear of the bar room and you can see a stillage with a few casks of beer sitting on it. Find a seat around the large square table and landlord John Rees (who is likely to be sitting amongst you) will take your order from a limited range of drinks. Please note the wit of John Rees is not for the faint hearted! The pub has been in his family since 1871 and very little has changed in that time. There was another public room – the smoke room – which is on the left of the passage and has a '1' on the door but it is no longer in use and is used for storage. Only open Fri. from 5.30 to 10.30; Sat. from 12 to 2 and 7 to 11; but it may close early.

You stand at the doorway to the cellar to be served at the Red Lion, Llandovery.

Right: The public bar of the Red Lion, Llandovery, is a simple affair with dado panelling and movable tables and seats and a fireplace. One bench has a high back and there is no counter.

Llanelli
Glyncoed Terrace, Halfway
SA15 1EZ
01554 773571
www.halfwayhotel.co.uk
Not listed
110/111/112
10 rooms in hotel and adjacent property (5 en-suite)
Meals (not Sun. evening)
Real ale most weekends, occasionally Welsh or guest

Halfway House

Rebuilt in 1894, the Halfway House has possibly the most impressive Victorian bar fittings in the whole of Wales. Built by local firm T P Jones, who also erected Llanelli Town Hall in 1896, it has a fine wooden gallery at first floor level with 'Halfway House' leaded panels. The impressive original bar counter and bar-back fitting take up two sides of the front left room. As well as displaying drinks they are full of items such as water jugs etc. with tall mirror fronted cupboards to each side. It is really pleasing to see how the original bar back fitting has been carefully preserved – even fridges have been added without destroying one shelf, and there are signs of recent restoration to the wood. The original counter curves at the front left-hand side as well as at the centre. The original interior of three rooms and a passage was, sadly, opened up by Bass in 1982. There is more elaborate ceiling decoration in the corridor to the rear. At the rear left is a dining room with modern brick bar and at the rear right a conservatory. The pub is incredibly busy when the Scarlets are playing in their new stadium, which is situated two minutes walk away and opened in November 2008. Live music in the bar after rugby matches. The pub has a bar skittle table and organises its own tournaments. Open all day.

The Halfway House, Llanelli has a fine exterior

The Halfway House, Llanelli has impressive Victorian bar fittings.

Meinciau
On B4309 SA17 5LE
01269 860247
Not listed
197 Llanelli–Carmarthen*
No food

**Despite the pub's restricted hours and somewhat remote location, the current bus timetable allows a visit of some 1¼ hours, during Saturday evening opening time only, from Llanelli direction only (no suitable return to Carmarthen). Please check before travelling!*

Black Horse

A three-roomed village local in the fifth generation of family ownership, it was last changed in the 1950s. A passage from the door leads to a bar in the centre of the pub. The main room in use is the small one at the front right with '1' on its sliding door and a 1950s brick fireplace. The panelling on the walls and the small bar were added in the 1970s – prior to that you were served through a door to the cellar behind. On the left of the passage a sliding door with '2' on it leads to what looks much like someone's living room although it does have a tiny quarter circle bar from the 1950s in the corner. To the rear left is another small homely room with a settee. This was originally part of the butcher's business, which ran from the pub in the past. Outside gents'. The pub is only open from 7.30 to 11 on Tue., Thu. and Sat. and the owner is considering retiring so best to ring if planning a visit.

The rear bar of the Black Horse, Meinciau, has a 1950s curved bar with a red Formica top and behind it you can see the stillage where casks of beer used to be stored – originally there was a wall separating the 'cellar' from the rest of the serving area.

Rhosaman
On A4068 SA18 1DW
01269 825785
Not listed
X13 Swansea–Brynamman, X24 Swansea–Ammanford, 124/125 Ammanford-Ystradgynlais
5 rooms (2 en-suite)
Meals lunchtimes
Occasionally sells a Welsh real ale, but otherwise a keg beer (labeled as such) is sold by handpump.

Rose & Crown

The public bar on the left has what was one of the longest bar counters in Wales – in former days very useful to place dozens of pints of beer ready to quench the thirst of the miners at the end of their shift at three local collieries. Most of the original bar back with some rows of mirrored panels continues almost to the back of the room. On the right of the entrance is the former lounge, which is now less than half of its original size and only used for dining by B&B customers. A couple of original etched windows remain. Opens at 7pm on Mon.; opens lunchtimes and evenings Tue. to Thu.; open all day Fri., Sat., Sun.

The left side of the bar back at the Rose & Crown, Rhosaman, does not have a counter in front of it because it was shortened some six feet in the 1970s and on the right you can easily see the join!

Trapp
SA19 6TP
01558 822330
Not listed
Meals lunchtimes (not Mon.) and evenings
Welsh real ale

Cennen Arms

The impressive feature of this three-roomed pub is the glazed screen around the servery, one of very few left in Wales. Opposite a hatch there is a narrow snug with tongue-and-grooved panelling on the walls and pointed ceiling. Fixed seating runs down both sides and at the end is a small extension containing a dining room. The lounge bar at the front was two small rooms until 2000 and has a bar counter possibly added c1960 and fireplace of similar age. The public bar at the rear has bar fittings that could also date from c.1960 and a small extension containing a pool table. New Year's Day is the pub's busiest of the year with the local hunt starting from here at 11am and the pub opens from 8.30am serving Cawl (Welsh lamb stew) all day.

The rare surviving glazed screen around the servery at the Cennen Arms, Trapp. There is another at the Dovey Valley Hotel, Cemmaes Road (p. 81), and a more modest one at the Fox, Ysceifiog (p. 52).

CEREDIGION

Cardigan/Aberteifi
1 Castle Street/ Bridge End SA43 3AB
01239 615282
Grade II listed
🚌 550/X50 from Aberystwyth, 460/1 from Carmarthen, 412 from Haverfordwest
No food

Castle

A 200-year-old basic locals' pub still with stables at the rear. It has been in the same family since 1940 and was run by Nellie Hopkins, the longest-serving pub landlady in Wales at 62 years when she died in 2002 aged 92. Originally three rooms, the one at the front right has been used by the family as a living room for many years. The bar back fitting in the public bar includes a till drawer dating from the 1950s, which is the date of the brick fireplace. Note the remains of the glazed screen over the bar counter and the slopes of the door frame. At the rear is the lounge with an old stone fireplace and service via a door to the back of the bar. Open all day on Sat. and Mon., open lunchtimes and evenings Tue. to Fri.; open lunchtime only on Sun.

The public bar on the left of the Castle, Cardigan still retains its Victorian bar counter but it has a frontage added in c.1980, which is the date the dado panelling was added to the room.

Llanddewi Brefi
SY25 6RS 01974 298452
Not listed
585 Aberystwyth–Lampeter
4 rooms
Meals (not Mon. lunchtime)
Welsh or guest real ale

The original pub room at the New Inn, Llanddewi Brefi, was the snug on the right of the photograph. The present main bar on the left is a conversion of a small second public room with part of the living accommodation carried out in 1987.

New Inn

The splendid unaltered snug on the left was the original public room and this was a 'no bar' pub until 1964. The tiny room has an old flagstone floor with some quarry-tiles near the fireplace, old panelled dado on the walls, one small wall bench on the window side, and a range fireplace as it originally doubled up as the licensee's kitchen. Beer would have been carried from the cellar in jugs until a little bar counter was added in 1964. The main bar has an early 20th century tiled, cast iron and wood surround fireplace in the left hand half i.e. the second room that was only used for special occasions such as the village Eisteddfod. A Breconshire real ale alternates with Timothy Taylor's Landlord and they are served from a polypin 'out the back' so please ask for real ale as there are few indications that it is on sale. Open 11 to 4 (not Mon.); 5.30 to 11.

TRY ALSO

The **Friendship Inn**, High Street, Borth SY24 5JA has been an inn since 1860 and in the same family since 1921. The public bar at the front was two small rooms until a partition was taken away in the 1980s and contains two sections of possibly Victorian fixed seating and a bar back fitting from the late 1950s. Note the Lichfield City Brewery Co. mirror. The former off sales compartment remains. The rear bar, now 'Sarah Pugh's Gallery', retains a 1960s bar back and bar counter with Formica top; also a 1920s fireplace. Upstairs is Above Stairs Antiques, a well-stocked collectables/bric-a-brac shop open for purchases from 11am to 5.30pm in summer and by appointment in winter. 01970 871213; www.friendshipinn.fsnet.co.uk; Guest real ale.

Tregaron
The Square SY25 6JL
01974 298208
www.talbothotel-tregaron.co.uk
Grade II listed
585 Aberystwyth–Lampeter
15 rooms (10 en-suite)
Meals lunchtimes and evenings
Real ales regularly including one Welsh

Talbot Hotel

A late 18th century drovers' inn with three rooms including a characterful snug. It was extended in the late 19th century with the arrival of the railway to Tregaron. The small lounge on the far left, with a flagstone floor, has a bar counter dating from c.1965 and bar back shelves possibly of similar date. Through a low doorway is the public bar at the rear with another c.1965 bar counter and bar back shelves, which replaced the original small counter on the opposite side of the room. In the hotel part there is an office/reception room, originally a private bar for the well-to-do locals, that has a colourful Victorian floor and curved partition walls. To the left of the passage with an 'Old Worthington in Bottle' mirror there is a small dado panelled room to the left, and on the right a room with two tiled fireplaces that until 50 years ago was two small rooms. Very busy when the Tregaron Trotting Club (www.tregarontrotting.com) holds its Spring meeting and three days of racing over the August bank holiday called the Festival of Harness; also for Ffair Garon on Spring Bank Holiday Monday. Open all day.

The public bar at the Talbot at Tregaron, which started life as a drovers' inn.

The flagstone floored and beamed front snug at the Talbot Hotel, Tregaron, with its inglenook fireplace including a bread oven and two antique settles is little changed since its days as a resting place for cattle drovers.

Drovers' Inns

The Welsh countryside is riddled with former drove roads created in medieval times as a vital means of transporting cattle, sheep, pigs and geese bound for market in England. Inns sprang up alongside these roads to provide refreshment and recuperation for the drovers and their charges. A number of these inns survive but the forlorn remains of many more can still be identified.

A classic example of a drovers' inn is the Rhydspence Inn (p. 92) right on the English border near Hay-on-Wye. The building dates from 1380 and may originally have provided comfort for pilgrims, but by the seventeenth century it had become a focal point for Welsh and Irish drovers on the Black Ox Trail from the Welsh uplands to the markets at Gloucester, Oxford and Smithfield in London.

Near Upper Chapel the small inn at Cwm Owen, astride the drove way to the Wye valley, finally succumbed as a result of the economic devastation wrought by the foot and mouth outbreak in 2001. Surviving drovers' inns elsewhere in mid Wales include the Talbot Hotel in Tregaron (p. 39) and the Red Lion at Llanfihangel Nant Melan east of Rhayader.

In north Wales a classic drovers route led eastwards from Anglesey, with cattle swimming the Menai Strait and then crossing the northern slopes of the Snowdonia massif before coming down by the Old Bull at Llanbedr-y-Cennin (p. 43) to the Conwy valley. Other drovers' inns in the north included the Sun (p. 50) at Rhewl near Llangollen, the community-owned Raven at Llanarmon-yn-Ial near Mold – sole survivor of ten inns in this important droving centre – and the thirteenth century Black Lion at Babell near Holywell.

Situated on a steep wooden hillside with splendid views over the Conwy valley the **Old Bull** at Llanbedr-y-Cennin started life as an important drovers' inn.

The distinctive Radnorshire style exterior of the **Rhydspence Inn**.

The small left hand room at the **Sun**, Rhewl near Llangollen

CONWY

Conwy
1–3 Uppergate Street, corner of Bangor Road LL32 8RF
Grade II listed
⇌ Conwy
🚌 all serving town centre
No food
Real ale usually from Brains

Albion ★

Re-built in 1921, this is by far the best surviving example of an interwar pub in Wales. It has three well-preserved rooms and the only significant change is the incorporation of the off-sales into the public bar (on the right-hand side). The exterior has a brick ground floor, and pebble-dashed first floor with a touch of Tudor half-timbering. The three splendid rooms are approached off a corridor with some attractive green Art Nouveau-style tiling in the dado and red tiling on the floor. Brown tiling in the lobby from the Bangor Road entrance. The new licensee has uncovered the door to the off sales (it had a dartboard over it) to reveal a 'Public Bar' panel in it. Public bar on the right with an original counter and fine mirrored bar-back incorporating a round clock by Parnell & Sons, Birmingham, and lots of shelves with columns holding them up, detail in wood relief and, thankfully, only a tiny section removed for a fridge. The bar fittings are looking much better now – the original stain was removed by a previous licensee and recently treated with linseed oil by the current one. The 1930s brick fireplace in the public bar has been painted black and the original parquet floor was removed in the 1980s. The plans for the rebuilding in 1921 are on the wall of the public bar and show that originally the door into the bar was

A partition with glass panels on the top once separated the off sales from the public bar in the Albion, Conwy. When removed in the 1970s the wood panels were added to the wall on the right side of the room and actually cover a tiled dado. You can see markings on the counter where the partition was fixed.

The rear Smoke Room of the Albion, Conwy is served via a hatch, which still retains its doors that can be closed. The smoke room has an impressive wide brick and tile fireplace, and still retains its original fixed seating, bell-pushes and a parquet floor with an unusual diamond shaped feature.

just inside the lobby, but moved further back by Ansells in the 1980s – hence there are no tiles on the right hand side of the lobby but they remain intact elesewhere. In the angle of the streets is a smoke room (now the pool room) with an impressive baronial-style fireplace set behind a timber and brick canopy. It retains its original seating still with the maker's label and bell pushes above, and Art Nouveaux stained and leaded oval shaped windows. Note the two semi-circular panels in the inner doors from the (disused) lobby 'Smoke' and 'Room', also a 'Smoke Room' panel in the exterior door. Behind the public bar is the snug with a 'Smoke Room' etched panel on the door that is mainly used for meetings. The present ladies' was the original gents – in 1949 an extension was added to create new gents' toilets.
Opens at 1pm (12 Fri to Sun).

TRY ALSO

In Old Colwyn the **Sun**, 383 Abergele Road LL29 9PL was built c.1844 and retains fittings from an inter-war refurbishment. This drinkers' pub has a bar that dates from the 1930s with a modern top although the bar back looks more of the 1960s with odd Formica shelves. To the left a wide arch has replaced the door to the small room, which has seating probably from the 1960s and copper top tables of a similar vintage, but the fireplace is modern. To the right is a 1930s partition, which has seen a panel removed to gain access to another small room, the original corner door having been blocked up many years ago. It retains one 'Vaults' window from the 1930s, fixed seating looks of a similar date, but the fireplace looks more 1960s. At the rear left past the cellar with a '3' on the door is a large long room which has been in use for many years and up to c.1990 there was a separate servery in here. 01492 517007; Real ale.

Llanbedr-y-Cennin
LL32 8JB
01492 660508
Grade II listed
19/X19 Llandudno–Llanrwst.
Alight Talybont and walk one mile
Meals lunchtimes (not Mon.)
and evenings
Lees real ale

The unusual feature in the Old Bull, Llanbedr-y-Cennin, is the bar back which incorporates a large 'Patterson's Scotch Whisky' mirror – something quite common in Scottish bars, but rare in Welsh (*and English*) ones. The present bar counter, which dates from the 1960s, has a log frontage and copper top and is set back a few feet from the position of the original bar.

Old Bull

There have been few changes to this late 17th century drovers' inn in the last 40 years. The oldest features are the partition to the right of the entrance with an unchanged bare bench attached and in the flagstone area beyond there is a massive stone fireplace taking up the whole of the right-hand wall. Originally there was a short passage and doors to both the right-hand side of the pub and into the left-hand side, which is on a higher level. The removal of the doors make the interior of the Old Bull, Llanbedr-y-Cennin look similar in style to many pubs, however, the amount of change is very little. A small dining room at the rear has been brought into use. Situated on a steep wooden hillside, there are splendid views over the Conwy valley from the car park and the pub is popular with bird watchers. Camping allowed in the paddock (up to five tents).
Open all day (in winter opens at 4pm Mon.).

In Llanrwst the **Pen-y-Bont**, a multi-roomed pub, is worth a visit. The two small bars were last refitted in c.1970.

Llanfairfechan
Mill Road LL33 0TH
01248 680584
Not listed
Llanfairfechan (train)
5/X5 Caernarfon–Llandudno (bus)
No food
Welsh real ale usually available

Passageway drinking at the Virginia Inn, Llanfairfechan – something which has virtually disappeared from pubs today. *Top right*: The right hand room of the Virginia Inn, Llanfairfechan.

Virginia Inn

Situated in a Victorian terrace of houses, this is a rare example of a traditional drinkers' pub with three small rooms and still with 'passageway drinking'. The front left small room is dominated by a large well-detailed inter-war brick fireplace; its Victorian bench seating is still in good order, and service is via a small bar which saw some changes in the 1960s with its Formica top and mirror feature around it. There is a fine 'Allsopp's Burton Ales' mirror over the fireplace. The right-hand room, originally the second public room in the past, was amalgamated with a former domestic room in the 1960s and contains a mixture of Victorian, post-war seating and some choristers' pews from an old chapel in Bangor. Look for the 'Abolish Slavery' on the legs of the Britannia tables in this room – Slavery was officially abolished in most of the British Empire on 1st August 1834. Outside gents' and ladies'. Next door to the pub is The Forge, the former blacksmiths, which is still in business as makers of wrought iron work. Pub is open all day from 12 apart from Sun. 12 to 3; 7 to 11. In January, February, and March closed Mon., Tue., and Wed.

Llanfihangel Glyn Myfyr
On B5105 LL21 9UL
01490 420209
Grade II listed
No food
Welsh real ale

Crown Inn

The door of the Crown Inn, Llanfihangel Glyn Myfyr, will remain open if customers old and new support it so please pay it a visit soon!

Pubs like this are closing at an alarming rate – this is run more as a hobby. Please don't let the limited hours put you off from a visit – it is worthwhile to visit a pub where good conversation and good beer are still the order of the day. A late 18th century building dramatically situated under a crag on a sharp bend. A Welsh slate passage runs down the centre and through a sliding door on the right is the small public bar with a counter and bar back shelves which look as if they could have been here since the 1950s. Until then there was no bar and beer was fetched from the cellar and served from a jug. On the left is the games room with bench seating and a pool table. Opens at 7 Thu. & Fri.; opens at 2 Sat. & Sun.; closed all day Mon., Tue., and Wed.

To accommodate the counter added in 1950 at the Crown Inn, Llanfihangel Glyn Myfyr, the original stone fireplace was blocked up and a new one created a few feet along the right hand wall; there is basic bench seating.

Llansannan
LL16 5HG
01745 870256
Not listed
48 Abergele–Llanrwst
2 rooms
Meals Sat. and Sun. lunchtimes and evenings
Lees real ales

Red Lion/Llew Coch

A visit to the Red Lion is 'a must' to see the tiny snug – an example of how many a traditional Welsh beer house looked prior to the late 1880s and the introduction of bar counters. In the old days the publican fetched the beer from the cellar and brought it direct to your seat. Nowadays you walk around the outside of the settle to go to a hatch for service. Old fittings include some shelves for a bar back. Up to 40 years ago the room at the rear was just the left hand half with its stone fireplace. In the 1960s it was doubled in size when the house next door was purchased by Lees Brewery of Middleton Junction, Manchester which enabled indoor toilets to be added and the front pool room was created which still retains a period bar counter. Holds a music event on the second weekend in July; and also busy on August bank holiday Mon. when the Llansannan Show is held. Opens at 4pm Mon. to Fri.; Open all day Sat., Sun.

The left-hand door of the Red Lion, Llansannan, leads into a domestic-looking room with a grandfather clock in the corner. On the right of the room is a curved settle with iron stays from the top of the settle to the beams above.

DENBIGHSHIRE/SIR DDINBYCH

Corwen
Bridge Street (A5) LL21 0AH
01490 413188
Grade II listed
5 from Wrexham, 51/X51 from Rhyl, X94 Wrexham–Barmouth
6 rooms (1 en-suite)
Meals lunchtimes in summer

Crown Hotel

This 17th century coaching inn was rebuilt in the early 19th-century as a hotel to serve the London-Holyhead turnpike road. It has two wood-panelled rooms from a quality refit in the 1960s. Note the 'Crown Hotel Garages' raised lettering in stone on the fascia – this was an early motor garage. The bar fittings could date from the 1960s or later and recently a small section of the panelling was removed and the tiled and wood surround fireplace replaced by a modern one. A room at the rear contains a pool table but no old fittings. In summer open all day. In winter opens at 5 Mon., Tue. and Thu.; open all day Fri., Sat. and Sun; may be open Wed. evening if football on TV.

The public bar of the Crown Hotel, Corwen, was refurbished in the mid-1960s involving adding wood-panelling all around the room.

Cyffylliog
LL15 2DN
01824 710664
Not listed
3 rooms (2 en-suite)
Meals Sat. & Sun. lunchtimes and evenings (not Tue.)
Lees real ales

Red Lion

This old village pub had a most unusual refit just after the war and materials used include items from demolished houses in Liverpool. It has four rooms and the toilets are 'must see' as well! The gents' accessed from the public bar has amazing walls of multi-coloured pieces of tiling from Victorian houses. The lounge bar has a 1940s large limestone and brick fireplace but the bar fittings are modern. A room on a lower level has another impressive fireplace and beyond that is what looks like someone's living room. Both the ladies' and gents' toilets here are worth a look with their walls of green Art Deco vitreous glass panels; the gents' has two massive urinals from the 1930s. To the left of the rear main entrance is another (dining) room also with a 1930s large limestone and brick fireplace. Opens at 4 Mon. to Fri., 12 Sat., Sun.

The nearest to a real heritage pub interior in Denbigh is the **Railway**, 2 Ruthin Rd LL16 3EL which still retains five small rooms, albeit with modern fittings. Sadly a partition was removed in 2006 so that the only item that is original is the terrazzo floor in the bar and lobby. Real ales.

The parquet floored public bar of the Red Lion, Cyffylliog, has a set of six leaded glass windows with inserts of different Welsh scenes, a large limestone and brick fireplace, and bar back fitting all dating from the 1940s; the bar counter is difficult to date but could be 40 years old.

TRY ALSO

In Graianrhyd the **Rose & Crown**, Llanarmon Road (on B5430) CH7 4QW consisted until c.1960 of just one room – the right hand bar – which had no counter, and beer was fetched from the cellar. Markings on the red quarry-tiled floor near the original door indicate the position of a short partition/screen. Then in the early 1960s the bar counter was added and the left-hand room, formerly private quarters, opened. It has a parquet floor, small brick fireplace from the 1950s and a counter added in the 1970s. This traditional country pub also has a small dining room opened in what was formerly a domestic area. 01824 780727; Real ales including Welsh.

Cynwyd
on B4401 LL21 0LD
01490 412450
Not listed
🚌 X94 Wrexham–Barmouth
No food

Prince of Wales

Multi-roomed village pub that has been in the same family since 1955 and is little-altered since the 1960s. The front door leads to the old off sales hatch with sliding windows and on the left a latch and plank door leads to the public bar. When Corwen Station closed in 1964 the landlady's father was a guard and on the window side of the room look for the stationmaster's chair, waiting room clock, bench seating and long table with 'GWR' on it that were purchased by him. Note the old cupboards in the wall either side of a brick fireplace from 1985. To the rear is the pool room, originally the kitchen, with a flagstone floor; also the darts area, which until 1985 was a separate tiny room. The lounge on the right with '4' on the door has bar fittings from the 1980s which replaced 1960s ones that themselves replaced a hatch. Fixed seating is from the 1960s. Open evenings only Mon. to Sat.; and all day Sun.

The public bar at the Prince of Wales, Cynwyd, has a curved counter from c.1960, which replaced a hatch. On the right is the off sales hatch, which is still in use by children buying sweets, crisps etc.

Wynnstay Arms Hotel

Llangollen
20 Bridge Street LL20 8PF
01978 860710
Grade II listed
🚌 5/5A from Wrexham, X94 Wrexham–Barmouth
🛏 5 (all en-suite); (also 3 Bunkhouses with 7 beds in each one)
Meals lunchtimes and evenings
Real ales

This is a traditional town hotel with four public rooms including a small unspoilt public bar. Probably built early 18th century this three-storey building has applied half-timbering added in 1897. In a typical Welsh style, access to the public bar would have been from the rear door and service to hotel customers would have been via the hatch in the door to the back of the bar. There is a small snug near the rear entrance that retains old fixed seating and also an outside gents'. To the left of the rear entrance is another drinking area around an old stone fireplace that has old fixed seating and an antique settle. Presumably there would have been a partition separating this from the snug. On the front left a room brought into pub use appears to have been refitted in the 1960s and has a pool table and behind it is a L-shaped dining room with a bare wood floor. The pub is very busy during the International Eisteddfod held in Llangollen in early July. Open all day.

The public bar of the Wynnstay Arms Hotel, Llangollen, has an old, possibly Victorian, counter, bar back shelving both ancient and modern, an inter-war Tudor arch shaped stone fireplace and old fixed seating possibly of similar vintage.

Why the Pubs in Wales Closed on Sundays

Heavy drinking in the early nineteenth century, partly fuelled by the increase in the number of public houses after the Beer Act liberalised licensing in 1830, inevitably led to calls for a more restrictive regime. By 1835 there were 25 temperance societies in Wales, originally placing an emphasis on restraint (for example the Aberystwyth Auxiliary Temperance Society urged abstinence from spirits and moderation in the consumption of beer) but later placing the emphasis on teetotalism, as with the Narberth Total Abstinence Society, founded in 1837.

Welsh temperance campaigners – supported by the strong Methodist traditions of the country – were undaunted, however, and triumphed in 1881 with the passing of the Welsh Sunday Closing Act. Astonishingly, until the late twentieth century it was illegal to buy a drink in a pub in Wales on a Sunday (clubs and hotels were exempt, and hence prospered). The introduction of local referenda in 1961 at last gave residents the opportunity to overturn this draconian legislation. Even so, it was not until 1996 that Dwyfor, the last district still observing Sunday closing, finally voted against the practice. Mercifully, these referenda were finally abolished in 2003.

Local landowners leapt onto the temperance bandwagon with alacrity: Lady Llanover, a devout Methodist and staunch teetotaller, turned Llanover village near Abergavenny into an oasis of Welshness in the 1840s, converting the Duke Inn into a temperance hotel. And somewhat improbably, the early headquarters of Abertillery Rugby Football Club were located in Buckley's Temperance Hotel in Oak Street.

Even more improbable were some of the steps taken to get around temperance restrictions. At Pontlottyn in the Rhymney

The **Temperance and Commercial** hotel at Newbridge-on-Wye.

Valley the teetotal landowner refused to allow public houses to be built in the village, but the Rhymney Railway Company allowed the Railway Inn to be built beneath three arches of their viaduct. Despite strong local opposition the Railway Inn was demolished in the 1990s.

Little remains of most of these havens of temperance although travellers on the A470 in mid Wales can still see the protruding porch of the former temperance hotel in Newbridge-on-Wye, with "Temperance and Commercial" etched in the glass of the porch.

This building looks like a pub but is in fact the **Coffee House**, Rossett, near Wrexham, which in recent times has been the Nat West bank.

Rhewl near Llangollen
On B5103 LL20 7YT
01978 861043
Grade II listed
98 from Llangollen (very restricted service)
2 rooms (can be bunkhouses sleeping 12)
Meals lunchtimes and evenings
Welsh or guest real ales

Sun

A splendid small three-roomed pub where the bar counter was only installed about 40 years ago; prior to that they would have fetched beer from the cellar. This drovers' inn is over 200 years old, deep in the countryside overlooking the Dee valley. On the left an old door leads to the lounge which is likely to have been a kitchen in the past with its splendid range fireplace and coal fire; it also has bench seating and a piano. Through a very low doorway – you have been warned! – there is a small area near a stable door for service with some old shelves beyond. In this area is another small room, which clearly had an inglenook fireplace at the rear in the past; it also has bench seating. Outside gents' and ladies'. There is a games room in buildings at the rear. Open all day.

The small public bar on the right at the Sun, Rhewl, has old half-height panelled walls and there was no bar counter until the 1960s.

The splendid range fireplace in the left hand room of the Sun, Rhewl.

FLINTSHIRE/SIR Y FFLINT

Cadole
Village Road (off A494) CH7 5LL
01352 810217
Not listed
6 from Shotton & Mold (only useful on Saturdays)
No food
Welsh real ales

Colomendy Arms

This small two-roomed drinkers' pub tucked away in a side road is barely changed since it was last refitted in 1962 and has been in the same ownership for over 20 years. The area in front of the bar has a Ruabon-tiled floor and the front part of the room bare boards, which seems to indicate it was two separate rooms prior to 1962. The front part has a small brick fireplace in a style seen around 1960 and the dado panelling is modern. The small lounge has a Ruabon-tiled floor and fixed seating, which appears as though it might date from c.1962; but the large fireplace looks much older. This traditional village pub with no food, no music, no pool and no machines still retains its outside gents' (with a covered walkway). Opens at 7 Mon., Tue., Wed; 6 Thu.; 4 Fri. ; 2 Sat., Sun.

The small bar at the Colomendy Arms, Cadole, has an early 1960s bar counter with a red Formica top and set of handpumps with the date of 1962; the bar back fitting is also from the 1960s and there are some older bar back shelves on the rear wall.

TRY ALSO In Shotton, the **Clwyd**, 28 Chester Road West CH5 1BY is a large 'brewers' Tudor' pub built as a railway hotel in the late 1890s, which still retains two small little-altered rooms on the right. The Commercial Room at the front retains original Victorian fixed seating. The rear right bar has bar fittings and seating from the 1950s. The rest of the pub, which was originally three rooms, was opened up, probably in the 1980s. Shotton Amateur Boxing Club uses the outbuildings. Grade II listed; 01244 813304.

Cilcain
The Square CH7 5NN
01352 740142
Not listed
14 Mold–Denbigh (some journeys only)
Meals lunchtimes and evenings
Real ales

White Horse

Multi-roomed old village pub, which in around 1940 expanded into the cottage next door and still retains the fittings from a refurbishment of that date. This is a pub that serves food and has no jukebox, pool table or children! Through an arch to the right of the bar is a small quarry-tiled room with c.1940 brick fireplace, and an antique settle, To the rear of this room is a tiny room with a grandfather clock and piano that is served from a small hatch to the back of the bar. From a separate entrance on the left is another bar created out of two small rooms of a cottage with a quarry-tiled floor, bar fittings and a brick fireplace from c.1940. The only changes are the adding of a copper bar top possibly in the 1960s; and in the early 1980s an extension was added to the rear of the right side adding a further room. At this time the bar counter was extended slightly to the right by adding an extra piece to the end near the fireplace. Open all day Sat., Sun.

On the right of the White Horse, Cilcain, the door with '1' on the inside leads to a small bar with quarry-tiled floor, this curved counter and an inglenook style fireplace which were all installed in c.1940.

The White Horse, Cilcain, was purchased and refitted in c.1940 out of Irish Sweepstake winnings!

Ysceifiog

The Village CH8 8NJ
01352 720241
Grade II listed
Meals from 6pm Thu. and Fri., 2pm (4pm winter) Sat. and Sun.
Real ales regularly including Welsh

Fox ★

This two-storey late Georgian village pub with four small rooms is a splendid survivor being little-altered since the 1930s. The slate-floored drinking lobby has a tiny hatch in the leaded screen around the servery, which would have also been the off-sales, and occasionally customers can be seen drinking here. A sliding door leads to the tiny front bar with an old counter, old panelling on the window side, a 1930's tiled fireplace with a coal fire and bare bench seating. The intimate space means visitors are quickly drawn into conversation. At the rear the lounge is served from a bar more like a hatch with its sliding window, now kept permanently open. This room retains fixed seating dating from the 1930s and a post-war fireplace. To the front right is the small snug with a cast-iron fireplace. Look for the number of the doors, a requirement of H M Customs and Excise to denote all the rooms in a public house used for the storage or sale of alcohol. There is a '4' on the door to the lounge; a '5' on the door to the rear right room, which has been in use as a dining room in the past; and '6' on the cellar door. Opens at 6pm Mon., Tue., Thu., and Fri.; closed all day Wed.; opens at 2pm on Sat., Sun.

The Fox, Ysceifiog, retains a disused, but rarely seen, cask pump – a way of serving beer direct from a cask with the added benefit of serving it with a good 'head' – if not visible just ask to see it.

The front bar of the Fox, Ysceifiog has bench seating attached to the front of the counter – something that may be unique in a pub anywhere.

TRY ALSO

The **White Lion**, Glan-yr-afon CH8 9BQ is a traditional pub still with its three-room layout. This was the childhood home of the dramatist and actor Emlyn Williams. The great survival here is the tiny snug in the rear middle part of the pub with old fixed seating and a half door for service. The original public bar on the rear left, now the lounge bar, still retains one of two original old settles around the fireplace. It was doubled in size in about 1984 by combining it with a former private living room and a bar counter was installed. The present public bar has an old stone fireplace but the bar fittings only date from 1984. 01745 560280.

GWYNEDD

Bangor
Platform 1, Bangor Station
LL57 1LZ
01248 364164
Grade II listed
Bangor
all serving city centre
Snacks

Snowdon Buffet & Bar

A rare example of an intact, simple station buffet, in this case probably fitted out in 1927 when additional station buildings were added. It has an elegant panelled counter and a pair of rather spindly, mirrored bar back fittings. The counter top is believed to have been marble originally and was probably replaced in the past 30–40 years, as the present one is Formica. Food is restricted to sandwiches, pasties, bacon & sausage baps, cup-a-soup and scones made on the premises. No draught or even keg beer – only cans, spirits from optics, a wide range of soft drinks as well as the more usual sweets, magazines, newspapers, tea and coffee. Open 5am to 5.15pm (6.15pm Fri.) Mon. to Sat.; 8am to 5.00pm Sun.

Bangor has the last surviving traditional station buffet bar in Wales, dating from 1927 – other remaining examples can be found at Bridlington, East Yorkshire, and Stalybridge, Greater Manchester.

Bethesda
Ogwen Terrace, London Road
(A5) LL57 3AY
01248 600219
www.douglas-arms-bethesda.co.uk
Grade II listed
7/67 from Bangor
No food
Welsh real ales

Douglas Arms ★

A coaching inn built c.1820 that has been in the same family since 1913 and is little changed since the 1930s with four public rooms. Tradition is the order of the day here – it was possibly the last pub to convert to decimal currency and even today staff can quote you the cost of your round in £sd. In the spacious corridor there is an old servery facing the front door. The public bar lies to the rear right and until the 1950s it was actually two small rooms but then a partition creating a separate snug was removed. What looks like a hatch on the left was actually the door into the snug and to access it from the hall there was originally a short passage across the corner of the servery.

The splendid over 100-year-old bar back at the Douglas Arms, Bethesda, contains many drawers, a display of spirit jars and 25 malt whiskies.

The public bar of the Douglas Arms, Bethesda – locals would use the door on the right-hand side of the building in the past, the front door being mainly used by hotel guests.

The Douglas Arms Hotel, Bethesda was built to serve Thomas Telford's new road to Holyhead

The public bar has two bentwood benches and a red leather bench; the now disused fireplace dates from the 1920s. Near the counter, which was re-fronted in recent times, there is the old speaking tube (now painted over), which was used to give instructions to the kitchen below. On the rear left is the billiard room, which is the combination of the former hotel reception and a room/lounge. The full-sized table was moved to here from an upstairs room in c.1934 and the rare game of Snooker Plus is played here – see page 22. The room has old bench seating, an early 20th century tiled fireplace (there was another behind the seating) and a hatch to the back of the bar. At the front are two rooms – on the left a small function/dining room which has a tiled and marble surround fireplace; on the right is the Smoke Room with a 1930s Art Deco wood surround fireplace that has a new tiled interior on a Welsh slate base, antique settles and lovely benches. The inside toilets were added in 1955. Opens at 5 Mon. to Fri.; opens at 3.30 Sat.; open 1 to 3.30 and 8 to 11.30 Sun, but seasonal variations so best to ring or check website.

Caernarfon
27 Northgate Street LL55 1RW
01286 673604
www.welsh-historic-inns.com
Grade II listed
All buses to town centre
15 rooms (all en-suite)
Meals 12 to 9pm
Real ales including Welsh

Black Boy Inn

This 17th century inn just inside the medieval town walls had a restoration in 1954 and the two bars are barely changed since then. In the centre is the lounge, which was a shop prior to 1954. The fine carved settles and chairs add to the character of the room and a line drawing on the wall confirms the fireplace is a replacement. The public bar on the left was two rooms prior to 1954 and has some genuine beams, an old stone fireplace at the front and 1950s brick one at the rear. The dado panelling and some seating could well date back to the 1950s, the unusual area above the servery is much older. The public bar counter is a replacement but in the same style as the one in the lounge. The dining room also has an old stone fireplace at the front but recently the 1950s brick one at the rear was replaced. A passage links the three rooms and has a quarry-tiled floor. In common with the town itself, the pub is predominantly Welsh-speaking. Open all day.

The lounge of the Black Boy Inn, Caernarfon retains its bar fittings from the 1950s. The chunky timber counter was slightly extended on the right in the 1970s and a new bar top was added.; the bar back shelves have a Formica covering.

TRY ALSO Also in Caernarfon the **Twthill Vaults** 'Y Twt Hill', 1 Thomas Street, corner Victoria Street LL55 1PB is of interest for its fittings from a 1930s refurbishment. This drinkers' pub has a portico entrance and splendid set of stained and leaded Ansell's windows including one of Caernarfon Castle. The male-dominated public bar retains its original fittings – the bar back with cupboard in it, bar counter, and possibly 1930s brick fireplace. The lounge has modern fittings. 01286 671430.

Corris
Bridge Street SY20 9SP
01654 761324
Grade II listed
🚌 34 from Machynlleth, or 32/X32 Machynlleth–Dolgellau and short walk. Evening service infrequent on both routes
Meals evenings
Welsh real ales

Slaters Arms

This three-roomed village pub built c.1860 has a rare feature – a very active intact off-sales. The slate floored area is situated just inside the door with service via a sliding hatch window and an old shelf opposite. It is popular with children buying sweets displayed in the window alongside, but there are still some customers who buy take away drinks! The main room on the right retains an old bar counter but new panels have recently been added to the front, and a new top has replaced the Formica one added in the 1960s. Some bar back shelves may be old as is the wide arch over the counter. This small room has a massive

The Slaters Arms, Corris, was recently bought by Celt Experience Brewery, who have exposed the slate floor in the main bar on the right.

inglenook style fireplace with a high mantleshelf held up by six decorative brackets, a brick interior and a coal fire. In the past the main public bar was the only room but a small lounge on the left was added and last modernised in the 1960s. Also in the 1960s the rear former private quarters were converted into what is now the pool room, which has a lino-tiled floor and slate fireplace. Folk music 1st Wed. of the month. Opens at 5pm – may open earlier in summer so best to ring to check.

Dinas Mawddwy
Off A470 SY20 9JA
01650 531247
www.llewcoch.co.uk
Not listed
33/36 from Machynlleth/ Dolgellau (both highly infrequent)
6 rooms (4 en-suite)
Meals lunchtimes and evenings (not Sun. evening)
Real ales including Welsh

Red Lion/Llew Coch

An old drovers' inn with a splendid public bar that is little-altered since the 1960s but appears as though it could have been like this for much longer. This small room has some old bar back shelves and in 1965 part of a former decoratively carved dressing table was added in front (other parts of the dresser are above the counter in the passage and in the lounge). The pub was extended to the rear in the late 1960s to create a modern lounge bar (and further extended in the 1970s). This saw the removal of a tiny snug just behind the public bar. Since the hatch was added in the passageway in the 1960s this has become a popular place for drinkers. The pool room on the left was a private lounge and brought into public use in the 1980s.

The very traditional public bar of the Red Lion, Dinas Mawddwy, has a Victorian bar counter with a copper top that replaced a Formica one in 1963, a c.1935 brick fireplace under an inglenook with a log fire, a high-backed settle and another 'antique' settle; however, the terrazzo tiled floor was only laid in 1977.

The deeply rutted scrubbed table in the public bar of the Red Lion, Dinas Mawddwy, which is believed to be 400 years old.

TRY ALSO

The nearest to a heritage pub interior in Dolgellau is the **Torrent Walk Hotel**, Smithfield Street LL40 1AA. An 18th century hotel in the narrow town centre streets, it retains most of its multi-roomed interior with old fireplaces, but the bar fittings date from c.1970. Note the good 'Coffee Room' etched panel in the door from the lobby to the right room. Grade II listed; 01341 422858; Welsh or guest real ale.

Nant Gwynant
At the junction of A486 and A4086 LL55 4NT
01286 870211
www.pyg.co.uk
Grade II listed
Snowdon Sherpa S2 Llandudno–Llanberis, S97 from Portmadog. In winter S2 runs Llanrwst-Llanberis only and both routes are less frequent.
16 rooms (5 en-suite) – please note Fri., Sat. & Sun. nights bookings must be for at least 2 nights
Meals lunchtimes (evening meals – see text)
Welsh real ale

Pen-y-Gwryd Hotel

Built in 1810 and situated high up in the heart of Snowdonia, this unspoilt inn was established in 1840 and has been in the hands of the same family since 1947. It has many mountaineering associations, not least memorabilia from the team who made the first ascent of Everest in 1953 and who used it as a training base. The theme is exemplified in the Everest Room on the rear left by an amazing Austrian alpine-style log-lined room, which was fitted out in the early 1950s and opened by John Hunt. Off the corridor are two other small public rooms with wide openings. The dining room is on the right with a tiled fireplace. A five-course dinner is provided for residents (and non-residents, if booked) at 7.30pm and is still announced in the traditional way by a gong. There is also a residents' lounge and a games room for residents with pool and table tennis. There is a family chapel at the rear of the hotel built in 2000. Services are held and at quiet times please ask the bar staff if you want to take a look. Opens at 9am for coffee; bar opens at 11am. In January and February the hotel is only open all day Fri. and Sat, and until 4pm Sunday. In November and December the hotel is closed.

The Everest Room of the Pen-y-Gwryd Hotel, has the signatures of Hillary, Hunt and most of the team that made the first ascent of Everest in 1953 and other notable visitors to the hotel such as actor Anthony Hopkins. *Below*: The original Smoke Room situated behind the serving counter is now a bar for residents only.

TRY ALSO

Tafarn-y-Plu, at Llanystumdwy LL52 0SH near Criccieth has three small rooms and was last changed in the early 1950s when a flat-roof extension was added and the rear bar created. The original public room is the small front quarry-tiled bar. The bar back and brick counters date from the 1950s. On the left of the front door former living quarters are now a dining room. The eminent statesman David Lloyd George was brought up in Llanystumdwy and the village has a Lloyd George Museum. Present owners support all things Welsh – on taking over they changed the pub name from the Feathers; and it holds conversational Welsh classes every Mon. 01766 523276; www.tafarnyplu.com/english/home.html; Two Welsh real ales.

The Great Welsh Brewing Revival

There has been an astonishing growth in the number of independent breweries in Wales in the last few years. The confidence of these micro-brewers to experiment with new and exciting recipes offers drinkers a richly rewarding experience in an increasing number of pubs. The *Good Beer Guide 2010* lists 42 breweries in Wales, compared with 17 only five years ago and a mere six in 1985.

Only two of the established independent brewers in Wales, Brains and Felinfoel, have survived, while others such as Buckleys in Llanelli (taken over and closed down by Brains), Crown in Pontyclun and the idiosyncratic Border Breweries of Wrexham have all bitten the dust. Some of the micro-brewing pioneers have also failed to last the course, among them the much-lamented Dyffryn Clwyd brewery, makers of the outstanding Pedwar Bawd (Four Thumbs) bitter, Samuel Powell's in Newtown and Silverthorne's in Gwent.

The **Wern Fawr**, Ystalyfera (p. 68) is the brewery tap for Bryncelyn Brewery.

The New Wave

Among the older established new wave brewers are Swansea Brewery, the first commercial brewery in the district for 30 years, whose beers provide a compelling reason to visit the Railway, Upper Killay (p. 103); Tomos Watkin, founded in 1995 in Llandeilo but now brewed in Swansea; Bullmastiff, operated as a craft brewery since 1987 but rarely available in the Cardiff area; and Plassey, established in 1985 and supplying 30 regular outlets including three on the leisure park south of Wrexham where the brewery is located.

A number of the new breweries were established to provide home brewed ales for one pub only, including the Bryncelyn Brewery that brews excellent beers with a Buddy Holly theme, Carter's at the White Hart, Machen (p. 18), which brews only for special occasions, Heart of Wales Brewery at the Neuadd Arms (p. 78) in the quirky little town of Llanwrtyd Wells, the tiny Gwynant Brewery at the Tynllidiart Arms, Capel Bangor near Aberystwyth; and the ultra-modern Zerodegrees brewery in Cardiff.

Other recently established breweries have loftier ambitions. Otley near Pontypridd have three pubs, an original approach to marketing based on O for Otley, and have won many awards, with O1 and O-Garden winning CAMRA's 2008 Champion Golden ale and Speciality Beer categories respectively. Breconshire, too, has three pubs and their golden ale Cribyn was CAMRA's Champion Best Bitter for 2009. Facers in Flint, owned by an ex-head brewer of Boddingtons, and Evan Evans in Llandeilo are other brewers who are expanding rapidly.

Beer Festivals

Most new breweries, however, count on sales at CAMRA beer festivals – with a chance of winning awards to promote their products to a wider audience. The ultimate accolade is to win Beer of the Year at the Great Welsh Beer and Cider Festival, which is held each June in Cardiff, but there are a host of smaller and more intimate festivals throughout Wales, including

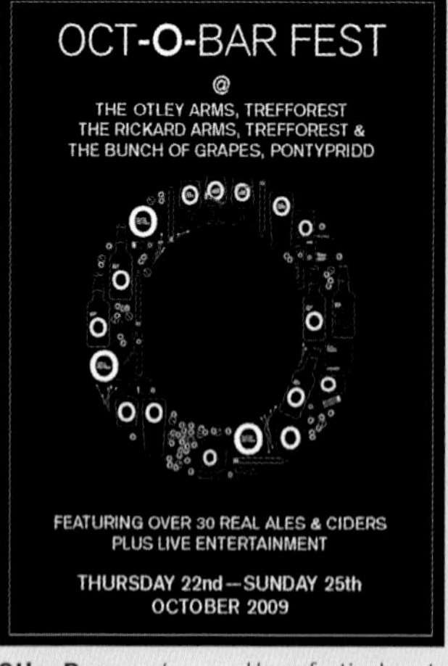

Otley Brewery's annual beer festival poster.

Swansea in August; Carmarthen in late Sept/early Oct; also one at Tredegar Park, Newport in May. The wackiest is the Mid Wales Beer Festival held in the three pubs of Llanwrtyd Wells who combine to offer more than 100 real ales each November.

A perennial award winner at these festivals is the Purple Moose Brewery (Bragdy Mws Piws), established in Porthmadog in 2005 and now supplying its much-feted beers such as Cwrw Eryri/ Snowdonia Ale, the Champion Beer of Wales 2009, and Ochr Tywyll y Mws/Dark Side of the Moose (Champion Winter Beer of Britain 2008) to over 100 outlets.

Cwrw Eryri/Snowdonia Ale, the Champion Beer of Wales 2009.

Beer Tourism

The growing importance of beer tourism means that many new brewers offer brewery tours and an on-site shop, as with the Waen Brewery, established at Penstrowed near Newtown in 2009 and selling its quirkily named beers such as First of the Summer Waen direct from the brewery. Kingstone near Tintern sells its own beers directly to callers, while Monty's at Hendomen near Montgomery offers brewery tours and Gwaun Valley near Fishguard welcomes sampling and visitors at its brand-new plant on Kilkiffeth Farm.

Others, including the Penlon Cottage Brewery at Llanarth, North Wales Brewery at Abergele and Jolly Brewer in Wrexham, rely on farmers markets and food festivals for a substantial element of sales of their real ales in a bottle.

Where to find Welsh Real Ale

In each pub entry we indicate if the real ales on sale come from one of the micro breweries set up in Wales in recent years by using the wording "Welsh Real Ale(s)". "Guest Real Ale(s)" indicates that the pub usually sells beers from micro breweries in England and these pubs could be selling locally produced real ales in the future. If all the real ales on sale are from larger independent breweries such as Brains of Cardiff, Felinfoel of Llanelli, Lees and Robinsons we say so, and if a tied house sells guest beers from other breweries we add "& guest beer(s)".

If you want to enjoy more of the products of the new breweries in pubs in Wales then please ask licensees "Do you sell a local beer?" to create a demand for them. Thank you.

e pool room of the **Neuadd Arms** (p. 78) becomes a cellar for the Mid Wales Beer Festival.

A Felinfoel handpump is not always a guarantee of real ale!

Prior to ordering a Felinfoel beer on handpump, particularly in a tied house, we strongly recommend you always ask "Which of these beers is real ale drawn from a cask?" Double Dragon is usually served from a cask, especially when in a free house; however, the Felinfoel website confirms Stout is a cream flow beer drawn from a keg using a 'Shakespeare pump' that looks identical to a handpump.

MONMOUTHSHIRE/SIR FYNWY

Abergavenny/Y Fenni
7 Flannel Street NP7 5EG
01873 853613
www.sabrain.com/henandchickens
Grade II listed
Abergavenny
all buses to town centre
Meals lunchtimes and evenings (not Sun. evening)
Brains real ales and one guest beer

Hen and Chickens

This is an example of how an historic pub interior can be sympathetically treated when extended into a neighbouring property. An 18th century building with a 19th century shop front including two brass plates advertising 'Hen and Chickens Hotel & Restaurant' and 'Hen & Chickens Dining Room Hot Dinners Daily'. It still retains its original three rooms and an old bar back fitting when the pub combined with a former hairdressers to the right in 1999. However, the bar back fitting running along the window side is from 1999, and previously there was a settle by the entrance with its back to the window; the marble surround fireplace is old. At the rear the small snug with shop-style windows has been reduced in size by a new partition to create a passage to new gents' toilets – the gents' was where the ladies' is now and the ladies' was previously upstairs. On the left the former coffee room is now a lounge with few if any old fittings, but some of the numbers over the doors including a '8' on the cellar have been retained. Live jazz Sun. lunchtimes. Open all day.

The original mirrored bar back fitting remains at the Hen & Chickens, Abergavenny, but is now at right angles to the present counter. Prior to 1999 there was a small counter directly in front of it. It is not clear if the old counter has been re-used or a new one created in the style of the original.

Abergavenny/Y Fenni
37 Brecon Road NP7 5UH
01873 854759
Not listed
Abergavenny
all buses to town centre
Sandwiches Thu., Fri., Sat. lunchtimes
Real ales

Station

Little-altered town pubs like this with lots of small rooms are getting rare so visit it now! This Victorian porticoed busy locals' pub built close to the former LMS station, one of three stations in Abergavenny, has signs of an old off-sales hatch as you enter. Note the Edwardian etched 'Station' & 'Vaults' panels in the side door to the public bar. There is a small lounge on the right. A quarry-tiled passage runs from a hatch at the back of the bar to the rear and outside gents' toilets. Opens at 5 Mon., Tue., 2 Wed., 12.30 Thu., 12 Fri., Sat., Sun

In the small public bar of the Station, Abergavenny the original bar back shelving extends across the room but the counter was shortened in the 1990s when a gap was created on the left to give access to the three linked rooms at the rear.

Wheatsheaf

Llanhennock
NP18 1LT
01633 420468
Not listed
Meals lunchtimes (not Sun.)
Real ales regularly including one Welsh

The small snug bar at the Wheatsheaf, Llanhennock, is a real period piece from c.1960 with its hardboard-panelled walls, small bar counter with a Formica top and small brick fireplace. The bar back shelves may be a later addition.

Old village pub still retaining its traditional layout of two bars and an off-sales and little-altered for over 40 years. As you walk in the original off-sales hatch is still there complete with sliding window, but the dado panelling only dates from the 1980s. In the bar on the right there is a c.1960 brick fireplace in which you will find an open fire in winter and there is a dado of ribbed hardboard. However, the counter only dates from the early 1990s. Look for the Hancock's Brewery framed poster, and the ceramic huntsman on a barrel shaped horse, which is advertising material for the long-defunct Rhymney Brewery that closed in 1978 (A new brewery with the same name started producing real ales in 2004). Just beyond the ladies toilet there is a small meeting room, which has been brought into use. In the car park are a number of boules pistes and views of Celtic Manor Golf Club, venue for the 2010 Ryder Cup. A travelling theatre calls here one evening in both May and September to perform a play on the lawn. Opens all day (except Sun. in winter when it opens lunchtimes and evenings).

Llanthony Priory Hotel

Llanthony
NP7 7NN
01873 890487
www.llanthonyprioryhotel.co.uk
Grade I listed
Summer Sundays and public holidays only B17 from Hay-on-Wye
4 rooms
Meals lunchtimes and evenings
Felinfoel Double Dragon and occasionally another Welsh real ale

Wales is blessed with numerous abbey remains but few perpetuate the monastic tradition of beer. We can therefore highly recommend a visit to the 13th century Crypt Bar of Llanthony Priory. Deep in the two-bay vaulted undercroft it consists of two distinct areas of character. The bar counter on the left is at least 40 years old and was slightly moved about 20 years ago, which could be the date of the bench seating in the form of settles, and there is some inter-war panelling on the walls. As one would expect from such an ancient building you have to take a narrow

The bar of Llanthony Priory Hotel is situated in a 13th century crypt, part of an Augustinian Priory. The ruins of the priory are open all year.

If you avail yourself of the accommodation (or book a table for a meal) at the Llanthony Priory Hotel, you can drink in the splendid residents' lounge/dining room with a vaulted ceiling, early 19th century range fireplace, and antique settle.

13th century spiral staircase to the four bedrooms, one of which has a vaulted roof. Court House Farm alongside the hotel has a campsite with basic facilities and offers riding for both experienced riders and beginners (01873 890359/www.llanthony.co.uk) In summer the hotel is open lunchtimes and evenings from Tue. to Fri.; open all day Sat., Sun & bank holiday Mon. In July and August it is open all day Mon. to Sun. From Nov. to Mar. the hotel is open Fri evening, Sat. all day; and Sun. lunch only.

Monmouth/Trefynwy

Granville Street NP25 3DR
07596 060607
www.sabrain.com/old-nags-head
Grade II* listed
🚌 60 from Newport,
69 from Chepstow,
83 from Abergavenny,
416 from Hereford
Meals lunchtimes and evenings
(not Mon. eve, Sun. eve)
Brains real ale

Old Nags Head

Here you can drink in one of the east gate's two round towers, part of Monmouth's medieval town wall, which is incorporated into this pub. This is a mainly early 19th century four-roomed pub that last changed in the early to mid 1960s. The wall between the 'Studio Bar' and the passage was replaced with a low partition at the same time. Panelling

The small front 'Studio Bar' of the Old Nags Head, Monmouth, which had a bar counter installed for the first time in the early to mid 1960s, previously the room was served via a hatch.

on the wall is of various dates and has wall bench seating attached; the fireplace looks 1960s. The second bar has a similar counter so was installed in the early to mid 1960s, the fireplace and all the bench seating is from the 1960s, but the flagstone-like floor is modern. The almost circular 'Gate Room', the old round tower, has modern panelling and floor. To the rear on a lower level is another small room with bare wood floor and old panelling that is now used as a dining room. The pub has been extended and includes a separate games room. Live bands are planned for Fri. nights.

TRY ALSO

Down the road the **Queens Head**, 1 James Street, Monmouth NP25 3DL is a timber-framed building of c.1630 that was extensively restored in 1922 and retains a number of old fittings. It has a splendid deep relief plaster ceiling; a post and panel partition; and large inglenook fireplace, but the bar fittings are modern. 01600 712767; www.queensheadmonmouth.co.uk; Real ales.

Monmouth/Trefynwy
Old Hereford Road NP25 3GA
01600 772505
Not listed
60 from Newport,
69 from Chepstow,
83 from Abergavenny,
416 from Hereford
Meals lunchtimes and evenings
Real ales

Royal Oak

The public bar of this food-led pub was refitted in the late 1950s and has barely been changed. The bar counter, wood-backed fixed seating with two baffles and stone fireplace all date from the late 1950s, the only change being a new wood top on the old Formica one, which remains. Note the old Bass Blue Triangle glass fronted sign on the wall. To the right an arch leads to a room which was extended by removing a wall and fireplace. The front section retains a two door leaded glass panel hatch to the side of the bar with a Formica top and old bare bench bay window seating. There is a two-part dining room on the left with no old fittings. The function room on the right can be converted to a skittle alley. Open all day Sat.

The 1950s bar back of the Royal Oak, Monmouth, has 'Whitbread' illuminated panels at the top, a glass block backing and some Formica shelves. Most fittings such as these have been ripped out of pubs in recent years making this one a rare survivor.

TRY ALSO

Whilst in the Monmouth area take a look at the **Boat**, Lone Lane, Penallt NP25 4AJ. To visit the pub you park in Redbrook next to the football ground on the A466, i.e. in England and cross the River Wye into Wales via the footbridge attached to the disused railway bridge! Prior to the 1960s this pub consisted of two tiny rooms each with a counter and occupying only the rear section of the present bar – note the two fireplaces. The front section including a separate snug was built on c.1965, the two rooms were then knocked into one and the present counter installed. Casks of beer and a large range of traditional cider and perry are served from a stillage against the back wall of the pub which is built into the steep hillside behind and spring water comes out of the wall occasionally! 01600 712615; www.theboatpenallt.co.uk; Guest real ales; Real draught cider and perry including some Welsh.

Shirenewton
Usk Road (B4235) NP16 6BU
01291 641231
Not listed
63 Chepstow–Pontypool
Meals Mon. to Fri. lunchtimes & evenings; Sat., Sun. from 12 to 9
Real ales
Real draught cider

Carpenters Arms

The Carpenters Arms has probably more small rooms that any other pub in Wales. This stone building was originally a bar and carpenter's shop, later a blacksmith's. The original bar was the flagstone-floored room just inside the main door with its huge settle held in place by an iron stay fixed to the ceiling, and which creates a passage into the pub. The bar counter was added in the 1960s replacing the original service hatch. The rear 'Smithy Bar' has a flagstone floor and a Victorian-style fireplace. To the right of the original bar the former cellar at a lower level has been made into another small bar. The room to the far right has been brought into pub use in recent years. Two rooms to the left of the front door were, and still do look like, domestic rooms – the far one has a 1920s Tudor stone fireplace. A wonderful pub with the only downside being the amount of 1960s Artex on the walls!

The rear 'Smithy Bar' of the Carpenters Arms, Shirenewton, was created out of a blacksmiths shop in the 1960s and has a counter formed of church furniture.

The Rebirth of Welsh Cider

Welsh cider making has enjoyed a remarkable resurgence, and can now boast around 30 producers and an enviable reputation for high quality products. It is there to be enjoyed – seek it out!

In the mid-1970s Ralph Owen started making cider initially for his own consumption. On moving in 1986 to his present Radnorshire base close to ample and under-exploited supplies of fruit he realised that cider-making could make a significant contribution to his overall farming business.

The crucial factor in the Welsh cider revival, though, was the formation of the Welsh Cider Society (later rechristened the Welsh Perry and Cider Society) in 2001 (www.welshcider.co.uk). For the first time ever, Welsh cider-makers had access to a support network offering valuable assistance and comradeship. No time was wasted in setting up an annual Welsh Perry and Cider Festival at the excellent Clytha Arms near Raglan in Monmouthshire at which the Welsh Perry and Cider Championships are judged.

And Welsh cider is second to none when it comes to quality. Set up in 2001, Gwynt y Ddraig cider, from the village of Llantwit Fardre near Pontypridd, quickly built up a reputation for both ambition and quality, so it was no great surprise when a gloriously complex and satisfying cider of theirs won the title of CAMRA's National Champion Cider of 2004. They then won the National Champion Perry award the following year – and in the same year, CAMRA's National Champion Cider was the intense, powerful 3Bs made by Ralph Owen!

Ralph's Old Badland was Champion cider in the early years of the Welsh Perry and Cider Championships.

In 2006, it was the turn of David Matthews' Seidr Dai perry to pick up the Champion Perry award, The impressive Blaengawney Cider picked up a bronze in 2008, and in 2009 small-scale producer Steve Hughes from Llandegla in Denbighshire gained joint silver in the cider class for Rosie's Triple D, while Seidr Dai won the silver award for perry with the delightful Painted Lady.

To find out more about cider and perry visit one of the growing number of Apple Day events that take place around the 21st of October annually including the National Trust properties Erddig and Llanerchaeron; St Fagan's National History Museum near Cardiff and the village of Cwmdu near Llandeilo.

The Welsh Perry and Cider Festival is held every late May bank holiday.

The **Boat** at Penallt (p. 64) has a range of ciders and perries.

Usk/Brynbuga
26 New Market Street NP15 1AT
01291 672931
Grade II listed
🚌 60 Newport-Monmouth
No accommodation
Meals lunchtimes and evenings (booking advised)
Guest real ales

Royal Hotel

The Royal Hotel built in 1839 is an example of how a pub when subject to sympathetic change can still retain an unspoilt feel. Popular with diners, the pub rooms were originally the two small ones on the right-hand side of the building beyond the fine shop front. The front door historically led to a passage to the rear of the building. The front right room was the bar and at the rear was a separate snug. Nowadays you will find an old bar counter placed across the passage in c.1960 and a bar back created behind it. The left bar was formerly two domestic rooms hence the range fireplace in the rear room indicating it was the kitchen in the past. The layout and fittings therefore only date back to the 1960s but the pub feels as if it has not changed for many more years. Note the one old penny billiard chalk dispenser on the front right mantleshelf. Open lunchtimes and evenings. Closed all day Mon., Closed Sun. eves.

The rear right area of the Royal Hotel, Usk, has markings on the ceiling which indicate the position of an antique settle that created a passage down the rear left side.

NEATH PORT TALBOT/CASTELL-NEDD PORT TALBOT

Pontardawe
High Street SA8 4JN
01792 862370
Not listed
Bus X20/120/125 from Swansea, X22/122/132 from Neath
No food

Ivy Bush

This is a big red-brick Edwardian pub that hosted the first public performances of Max Boyce, and Mary Hopkin, who was born in Pontardawe, started her career here. The function room upstairs is the home of the Valley Folk Club, which started 40 years ago. Performances are on 1st and 3rd Fridays at 8.30pm – more info. on 01792 863940 www.pontardawefolkclub.co.uk. The impressive entrance canopy on cast-iron columns leads into a quarry-tiled passage from the front door to the rear with Art Nouveau stained glass in the internal entrance lobby. The large bare boarded public bar on the right has 'Ivy Bush'

Right: The public bar of the Ivy Bush, Pontardawe, retains its fine Edwardian mirrored bar back fitting with columns holding up the shelves, and an original counter with a modern red Formica top.

The Valley Folk Club was formed 40 years ago and has performances in the upstairs function room of the Ivy Bush, Pontardawe, on the 1st & 3rd Fridays at 8.30pm – in the past these have included Max Boyce and Mary Hopkin.

and 'Bar' etched windows, old benches line two sides of the room, and there are red Formica tables but the old fireplace is covered by a radiator. On the left is the Commercial Room, which until the 1960s was two small rooms and has a bar counter, bar back and fixed seating all from the 1960s. At the rear is a small room, which is mainly used by the Swansea Valley Pigeon Club and has a trophy cabinet but no old fittings. The function room has a bare wood floor, fixed seating around most of the room and a 1950s tiled fireplace covered by a more modern one. Outside gents retains original urinals. Live music Sat. evenings. Opens at 4pm Mon. to Thu.; 2.30 Fri., Sat.; 11.30 Sun.

Ystalyfera

13 Commercial Street SA9 2HR

01639 843432

Not listed

🚌 125 from Swansea (change at Pontardawe). Stop is at junction of Commercial Street and Alltygrug Road, at/opposite newsagent's

No food

Red Cow

This Edwardian brick built locals' pub has a multi-roomed interior including an off sales hatch. On the left is the public bar with a couple of 'Bar' etched windows, the original bar counter with a red Formica top, and an original part mirrored bar back. An old wood surround fireplace is blocked up and the seating looks to be from the 1960s. On the right is the Smoke Room where another old wood surround fireplace is blocked up and there are 'Smoke Room' etched windows. At the rear is another small room with full height ply-panelled walls from c.1960 and which is popular for darts. There is a former function room upstairs (in use until 2007) and a series of small rooms in the basement. Opens at 4pm Mon. to Sat.; 1pm Sun.

The off sales hatch at the Red Cow, Ystalyfera, in the passage from the front door to the rear.

Ystalyfera
47 Wern Road SA9 2LX
01639 843625
Not listed
125 from Swansea (change at Pontardawe). Stop is at junction of Commercial Street and Alltygrug Road, at/opposite newsagent's
No food
Welsh real ales
Real draught cider

Wern Fawr Inn

The public bar still retains old bar fittings and something rarely seen these days – an old stove with the flue rising up from it and out through the exterior wall. Note the old till drawer in the bar back fitting; the old bar counter still remains but was moved back a few feet in the 1970s. There are some original etched windows on the front and old fixed seating. On the left two small rooms were knocked together in the 1970s and new bar fittings installed. This pub was the original site of the Bryncelyn Brewery, which commenced in 1999 and moved in 2007 to Ystradgynlais. Opens at 7pm Mon. to Thu.; 6.30pm Fri.; 2pm Sun.

In the public bar of the Wern Fawr Inn, Ystalyfera, the old stove nicknamed 'the Nuclear Reactor' was introduced in 1968 and is still in use most days.

TRY ALSO

The nearby **Ystalyfera Arms** ('Pig'), Cyfyng Road SA9 2BS has some unusual pub room names – the lobby has 'Hall' on the door as you enter. On the left two small rooms labelled 'Smoke Room Glasses Only' and 'Smoke Room' now have a wide gap in the wall to join them and the rear door is no longer in use. This drinkers' pub built 1830 has 'Bar' on the door on the right which leads to the small public bar that retains its original bar back (at least the top section); the bar counter is old but has a new top and in 2004 tiles were added over the old wooden frontage. However, both have been shortened by a few feet in recent years; and other 1960s fittings include a tiled fireplace and fixed seating. 01639 842301.

NEWPORT/CASNEWYDD

Newport/Casnewydd
Albert Terrace NP20 4BS
01633 213734
Not listed
Newport
All to city centre
No food
Real ale

Right: The snug at the Engineers Arms, Newport.

The Victorian public bar counter at the Engineers Arms, Newport

Engineers Arms

Victorian back-street local that still retains its little-altered small public bar and tiny snug. The public bar on the right is wedge-shaped as the building is in a fork in the road. It retains its original curved bar with the original top still in place but covered with newer wood. The bar back is a mixture of old and new (e.g. the mirrors); the dado panelling looks old but the seating looks like it was added in the 1960/70s. To the rear of the bar is the 'snug', which originally was a tiny separate room on the other side of an off sales corridor. It retains old bench seating either side of a c.1920 tiled and wood surround fireplace. On the left of the pub is the Middle Bar, and at the rear is the lounge, originally a tiny room served by a hatch. Both these bars were modernised in the 1970s, when the lounge was extended by purchasing the house next door, and they have no old fittings. This is a lively music venue at weekends with bands playing in the large bar. Open all day from 10am Mon. to Sat.; 12 noon Sun.

Newport/Casnewydd
113 Alexandra Road, Pillgwenlly, alongside A4042 Usk Way bypass NP20 2JG
01633 264266
www.thewaterloohotel.co.uk
Grade II listed
40
21 rooms (all en-suite)
Meals lunchtimes and evenings

Waterloo Hotel & Bistro Restaurant

Substantial Edwardian three-storey pub with one of the most impressive interiors in the whole of Wales including one of only two remaining tiled counters (the other is at the Golden Cross, Cardiff (p. 23). Rebuilt in 1904 mostly of red brick with terracotta detailing and impressive corner turreted clock tower, it is situated opposite the main entrance to Newport Docks. The entrance in Alexandra Road leads to a terrazzo-floored lobby/reception with a dado of green tiles and Queen Anne detailing on the staircase. To access the large public bar an arch was cut

The main bar at the Waterloo Hotel & Bistro, Newport also with an impressive ceramic bar counter – note how the right hand half is missing!

The Smoke Room at the Waterloo Hotel & Bistro, Newport, with its impressive ceramic bar counter – one of only two in Wales (and one of only twenty left in the whole of the UK). It is of Doulton faïence in five sections separated by columns with decorative capitals in deep yellow with floral tiled panels in bright blue. This terrazzo-floored room retains its original mahogany bar back with mirror panels but the pot shelf is a modern addition.

into the dividing wall from the smaller smoke room in recent years; this leads to the large main bar and its original corner entrance has been blocked up. The terrazzo floor indicates there was a small separate room, possibly an off sales on the left side of the room. This retains its splendid original mahogany bar back lining two sides and an L-shaped ornately tiled bar counter. However, only half of the counter still remains, the other half having been removed and reputedly sold and shipped to America in the early 1980s. Note the etched windows (some replacements) announcing 'Vaults' and 'Workman's Dining Room' – the latter being the room on the left of the entrance lobby which operated as a snack bar with 1950s fittings until the pub closed in 2002. After renovations it reopened as the Waterloo Hotel & Bistro Restaurant in 2007. With no public bar facility, it is currently open to diners and residents; however, users of this guide are very welcome to call for a coffee during the lunchtime opening hours of 11am to 3pm in order to take a look around this splendid historic pub interior.

The mahogany bar back in the main bar at the Waterloo Hotel & Bistro, Newport.

PEMBROKESHIRE/SIR BENFRO

Amroth
On coastal road at east end of village SA67 8NW
01834 812368
www.designasite.co.uk/newinnamroth
Not listed
351 Tenby-Pendine
Food all day (not October to Easter)
Real ales regularly including one Welsh or guest

New Inn

Tucked away on the coastal road at the start of the Pembrokeshire National Park's long distance coastal footpath, this stone-built inn dating from at least c.1800 is little-altered in 50 years. At the rear the characterful snug bar has an old flagstone floor, massive inglenook fireplace with log fire and was probably a kitchen in the past and possibly dates back to the 16th century. The carved bar counter front and bar back shelves could be 50 years old. Partitions that separated the two front rooms have been removed and the area on the right has an old stone fireplace, three antique settles, an old 'Bass in Bottle' wall sign and the landlady's collection of miniatures in four display cases. Upstairs is a dining room with a Welsh dresser and a bar counter (now disused) at least 40 years old. A new dining room on the rear left was formerly a cellar. The pub is open all day Easter to the end of October, and then closed completely from November to Easter.

The counter in the front bar of the New Inn, Amroth, is believed to date from 1953 and incorporates parts from an old sea chest.

Angle
Angle Bay village SA71 5AS
01646 641205
www.theoldpointhouse.co.uk
Grade II listed
387/388 Coastal Cruiser from Pembroke (infrequent, especially in winter)
3 rooms (1 en-suite)
Meals lunchtimes (not Tue. in winter), and evenings (only Fri. and Sat. evenings in winter)
Please ask which beers on handpump come from a cask – Felinfoel Best Bitter is real ale but other Felinfoel beers are not and come from a keg!

The Old Point House

The early 18th century Old Point House has an unspoilt and spartan tiny snug bar, which until the 1980s was the only public room – now there are three small rooms. The approach to the pub is also unspoilt as you drive down an unmade road around Angle Bay, which can get cut-off by spring tides for up to one-and-a-half hours. Called the 'Lifeboatman's local' since the neighbouring lifeboat station opened in 1868. The beamed bar measuring 4m × 5m has a concrete floor, range fireplace, two fine old wooden settles and just one table. The bar counters may be 40 years old and have slate slabs for counter tops that were added in the 1990s. There are two other rooms each with a similar bar counter – the dining room on the rear right was brought into use in the 1980s; the lounge bar on the left was converted from living quarters in the 1990s. Recently, a former sitting room has been brought into use as a public room, when required. Outside gents' and ladies'. In summer open all day and closes at 10pm. In winter open lunchtimes and evenings; closed all day Tue. in winter.

The tiny unspoilt public bar of the Old Point House, Angle, where it is reputed that some of the ships' biscuits for Nelson's fleet were baked in the large oven that was situated adjacent to the 19th century cast-iron kitchen range.

Cresswell Quay
SA68 0TE
01646 651210
Grade II listed
🚌 361 Tenby–Pembroke Dock (infrequent)
The only food is filled rolls put on sale Sat. lunchtimes until they sell out!
Real ale

Cresselly Arms

Only the most minor of changes have been made to the unspoilt public bar of this out-of-the way pub, which remained in the Davies family from 1896 to 1981. This is one of only two pubs left in Wales where you are served beer in the most traditional of ways – from casks on stillage behind the counter into a jug and then from the jug into your glass – the other is the Dyffryn Arms, Pontfaen (p.77). This fine creeper covered 18th century house beside a tidal creek was remodelled and opened as a pub in the 1880s. Alice Davies ran it from 1961 until 1981 when she was in her 90s and the oldest licensee in the county. Maurice & Janet Cole took over in 1981 and looked after Alice Davies until she

The Victorian public bar of the Cresselly Arms, Cresswell Quay, looks little different to when it was opened in 1880 with red and black quarry-tiled floor, open cast-iron fireplace, Victorian counter and bar back shelves held up by slender columns. Seating includes basic benches attached to a half-height panelled dado.

A very traditional way to arrive at the unspoilt Cresselly Arms, Cresswell Quay.

died aged 105. The only change made by the Coles' has been to cut a narrow opening in the dividing wall to the former kitchen and pantry in c.1981 to expand the public area and slightly extend the bar counter. The rear area also has a red and black quarry-tiled floor and an Aga cooker with tiled surround. Note the door with a number '3' on it, which suggests it was a room used for storing alcohol (the numbering was a requirement of Customs and Excise for rooms for serving or storing alcohol). To the rear right is a further room, which has been brought into public use in recent years. It has an early 20th century tiled and cast-iron fireplace and glass-fronted display cabinet. Gents' accessed via passageway – the original outside gents' are still there! Open 12 to 3; 5 to 11; Mon. to Fri.; 12 to 11 Sat.; Sun. 12 to 3; 5 (7 winter) to 10.30.

Fishguard/Abergwaun
24 Main Street SA65 9HQ
01348 872763
Grade II listed
Fishguard Harbour (very limited service)
412 Haverfordwest–Cardigan
Snacks
Real ale

Fishguard Arms

A very traditional pub hidden in an early 19th century terrace near the centre of town that looks more like a house, and still sells beer from casks behind the bar. A passage runs down the left side of the interior and at the front of the pub is a very traditional small bar where good conversation is the main draw. It has a bare wood floor, a 1930s bar counter, old bar back shelves, wood-panelled ceiling, casks of Bass on a stillage, old dado panelled walls and a log fire. At the end of the passage is another bare-floored bar with wood-panelled walls of various ages, a more modern bar counter, a new brick fireplace and an old basic bench. The outside gents' and ladies' are now under cover. Up seven steps is the recently created 'sky lounge' with tables and heaters for smokers and anyone else who wants to join them! Anyone asking for food may be directed to a local chip shop – it is owned by the licensees but leased out. You can eat your fish and chips etc. in the pub, with a cup of tea or coffee if you prefer! Opens at 4pm Mon., Tue., and Wed.; Open all day Thu. to Sun.

The Fishguard Arms, Fishguard, is hidden in a terrace near the town centre.

On the ceiling in the public bar of the Fishguard Arms, Fishguard, are the beer prices for the period 1982 to 1988 – a pint in 1982 was 52p and in 1988 was 92p, an increase of 77% in just 6 years whereas whisky rose from 45p to 62p i.e. only 37%!

Service in a Welsh Pub

Nowadays a customer expects to walk to a bar counter to be served. Yet the counter is a Victorian invention, with the earliest known examples dating from the 1860s.

Beer From The Cask

There are, however, still some examples in Wales of how customers were once served. Many pubs were just one simple room and the licensee fetched the beer from the cellar (where the beer was stored to keep it at a steady temperature) and brought it to your table. This still happens at the Red Lion, Llandovery (p. 34), which has no bar counter.

The traditional way of serving beer illustrated by the **Fishguard Arms**, Fishguard (p. 73) – direct from the cask into your glass.

The very traditional way of serving beer still seen today at the **Cresselly Arms**, Cresswell Quay (p. 72).

Another pub which has just a single room and cellar with no bar, but just a hatch is the Dyffryn Arms, Pontfaen (p. 77), Here the way of serving the real ale is also old fashioned – firstly the beer is drawn from the cask into a jug; then the beer is poured from jug into the glass.

Table Service

You can still spot bell pushes on the walls of Welsh pubs. They are a reminder of the once-common practice of table service. When the bell was rung it triggered an indicator in a bell-box that was visible to bar staff, who would then come to your table to take your order. The original bell pushes (sadly no longer in working order) can still be seen at the Albion, Conwy (p. 41). We are not aware of a pub in Wales still offering table service using bell pushes.

Bell pushes at the **Lion Royal Hotel**, Rhayader (p. 90).

Service Via a Hatch

Another traditional way of getting service is via a hatch rather than a bar counter and good examples can be seen at the Fox, Ysceifiog (p. 52); and Albion, Conwy (p. 41), both still with their doors; Douglas Arms, Bethesda (p. 53); and Crown & Anchor, Llanidloes (p. 85) amongst others.

The intact hatch at the **Albion**, Conwy (p. 41)

The splendid set of service bells in the Bell Bar of the **Neuadd Arms**, Llanwrtyd Wells (p. 78) is one of the finest sets left in a hotel/pub in Wales. These date back to the time this room was the kitchen and they were used to call staff for hotel service.

On the right-hand side of the **Bowling Green**, Wrexham (p. 111), is this (now blocked up) door with wording in stone relief.

Off Sales

In the past an active part of pub trade was drink bought for consumption off the premises, commonly known as 'Off Sales'. The sales would be from a separate small room or a hatch just inside the pub entrance as the purchasers were often women, even children, who were sent to the pub to collect the family supplies. The requirement of separation was to shield them from seeing men drinking in the bar.

Since the 1960s their importance has declined as people began to stop using the pub for take-home supplies and got them instead from off licences, supermarkets and France! Most of these tiny spaces have been absorbed into other pub rooms but there are some notable examples left. The off sales at the Slaters Arms, Corris (p. 55) is still active today and there are intact hatches just inside the Prince of Wales, Cynwyd (p. 47) and in the passageway of the Lamb, Penderyn (p. 96) which now act more as sweet shops for the children as shops have closed.

At the Witchill, Barry (p. 106) the now disused room is more like the size of a small shop and etched into the window glass is the wording 'Jug & Bottle Department', so named, of course, after the vessels used to take home the chosen liquor.

The off sales is just inside the door of the **Wheatsheaf**, Llanhennock (p. 61), complete with its intact sliding hatch windows.

TRY ALSO

In Narberth/Arberth the **Kirkland Arms**, East Gate, St James Street SA67 7DB is worth a look to see the traditional public bar with a quarry-tiled floor and Victorian bevelled mirrored bar back. The original servery was so large that there was more room behind the bar for staff than for customers so in the 1960s the counter was shortened in length. Note the still functioning 'Guinness Time' clock on the wall. In the 1990s the two left-hand rooms and passage were converted into one room. The pub was renamed after the horse that won the 1905 Grand National and rested here. 01834 860423; Please ask which beers on handpump come from a cask – Felinfoel Best Bitter is real ale but other Felinfoel beers are not and come from a keg.

Pembroke Dock/ Doc Penfro
20 Bush Street SA72 6AX
01646 680033
Not listed
Pembroke Dock
356 Pembroke–Milford Haven, 357 from Pembroke
3 rooms
No food
Welsh real ales

Charlton

Late Victorian red brick corner pub which retains splendid original bar fittings. One of a number of pubs built on the intersections of Pembroke Dock's Victorian grid-iron-style streets. Each had long bars for lines of drinks ready for the influx of thirsty dockyard workers when the evening hooter blew (the naval dockyard closed in 1926). A drinkers' pub, it only reluctantly allowed females onto the premises in the 1970s when it was forced to do so by law! The public bar has original dado panelling, colourful patterned glass in the lower parts of four windows, and old bench seating, but the vestibule entrance is more modern. Beyond this room on the Park Street side are two rooms – first a small lounge and then a larger pool room at the rear with openings to the left and right between them. Apart from the odd colourful leaded window there are no old fittings. Even the original outside gents' survive with their four large Twyford's Adamant urinals, but now, for comfort, they have a roof over them! Open all day. May not open until later on Sun.

The small public bar at the front of the Charlton, Pembroke Dock, has an unaltered four-bay mirrored bar back and a sturdy Victorian panelled bar counter which curves on the left side.

Pontfaen
SA65 9SG
01348 881305
Not listed
No usable service
No food
Real ale

Dyffryn Arms ★

This is one of the greatest survivors among Britain's rural pubs and a reminder of how many thousands must once have appeared. There is not a bar counter as such – just an opening with horizontally-sliding sashes to the ground floor cellar that is opened for service and closed afterwards. The pebble-dashed building is dated 1845 and looks more like a house as there is no hanging inn sign, just a small one above the now disused original main door. The pub has been in the same family ownership since built and is affectionately known as 'Bessie's' after the characterful octogenarian licensee; Welsh language conversation predominates in this pub. The floor has red and black quarry tiles and there is a rough stone fireplace, which might have been introduced in c.1960. The beer is served via a glass jug into your glass – one of only two pubs in Wales still using this time honoured way of selling beer – the other is the Cresselly Arms, Cresswell Quay (p. 72). A second room, the lounge, which is sometimes brought into use, lies across a corridor from the public bar. The main entrance is now down a passage on the right in an attached building where the only feature that extends beyond the purely functional is the light brown and black dado tiling dating from 1938. Almost without exception, pubs are now stand-alone businesses but here at the Dyffryn Arms, the pub is still linked to a smallholding with ten acres of farmland plus six of woodland. Outside gents' and ladies'. New Year is celebrated here on the 13th January – this is the only time you will see food in this pub! There is also a charity event on the Saturday of the May bank Holiday weekend with stalls outside the pub. It is usually open from 11am to 12midnight, but may close at 10 if there are no customers; open 12 to 10.30 Sun.

Beer at the Dyffryn Arms, Pontfaen, is stillaged just behind the hatch in the simple cellar.

The heart of the Dyffryn Arms, Pontfaen, is a squarish public bar with a medley of furniture including an old high-back seat/box settle and a low basic bench – there is virtually nothing to distinguish this from an ordinary domestic room.

POWYS – BRECKNOCKSHIRE/POWYS – SIR FRYCHEINIOG

Builth Wells/ Llanfair-Ym-Muallt
1 West Street LD2 3AH
01982 553648
Grade II listed
🚌 704 Newtown–Brecon
Meals lunchtimes (may extend in summer)
Real ale

Barley Mow

18th century town centre pub that had a refit in the 1930s and still retains some fittings from that period including parquet floors, some panelling, doors and fireplaces. The bar on the right saw changes in the early 1960s, which is the date of the bar counter and bar back. Through a gap in a timber and glass partition is another small room. On the front left, where there is now a hatch/doorway, a small bar was removed in the early 1980s, the two small rooms combined, and a new bar counter added at the rear. Open all day.

The right-hand room at the Barley Mow, Builth Wells, has a parquet floor, old dado panelling, a hatch to the side of the bar, but a modern fireplace. *Below:* The entrance lobby of the Barley Mow, Builth Wells.

Llanwrtyd Wells
The Square (on A483) LD5 4RB
01591 610236
www.neuaddarmshotel.co.uk
Grade II listed
🚆 Llanwrtyd Wells
🚌 48 from Builth Wells (infrequent)
🛏 21 rooms (all en-suite)
Meals lunchtimes and evenings; also breakfasts for non-residents
Heart of Wales home brewed real ales
Real Welsh draught cider

Neuadd Arms Hotel

The Bell Bar, with its own entrance on the left side of the building, created in c.1950, was originally the hotel kitchen and is virtually unchanged since. It is so named as on the walls are 18 service bells – the second best display of high Victorian service bells in a UK pub/hotel (the Royal Castle Hotel, Dartmouth has 43). The small room has a black and red quarry-tiled floor, solid bar counter, bar back shelves and a large stone fireplace. Beyond the bar is a quarry-tiled pool room, formerly an extension to contain the new kitchen, which still retains its range fireplace and has the pub game of quoits. The part Georgian, part early Victorian three-storey hotel has a lounge bar with a velour padded bar front, bar back shelves and stone fireplace which all look very late 1960s. There is also a residents' lounge, restaurant and 21 bedrooms, as well as its own brewery at the rear. The Neuadd Arms Hotel is one of the three venues for the ten day Mid Wales Beer Festival in November over two weekends including the 20th, and the pub holds its own Winter Warmer beer festival on the second weekend in January. Open all day.

The handpumps on the counter of the Bell Bar at the Neuadd Arms Hotel, Llanwrtyd Wells, dispense home brewed ales. *Right:* On the wall of the Bell Bar at the Neuadd Arms Hotel, Llanwrtyd Wells, you will see details of the winners of some of the large array of events that are held in the town, including the Man Versus Horse Marathon on the 2nd weekend in June; and the World Bog Snorkelling Championships in August.

Talybont-on-Usk
(on B4558) LD3 7YX
01874 676635
www.starinntalybont.co.uk
Grade II listed
X43 Cardiff–Brecon–Abergavenny
2 rooms (both en-suite)
Meals lunchtimes and evenings
Welsh real ales
Real Welsh draught cider

Star

A three-roomed pub popular with diners and drinkers, this late Georgian rendered building has a public bar on the left little changed in 70 years. You can arrive here by narrow boat as a series of steps and a steep slope lead up to the canal towpath of the Monmouthshire & Brecon Canal also used by walkers and cyclists. The small public bar has a red quarry-tiled floor, and bar fittings which look at least 1930s work. The old stone fireplace has a bread oven to the left, the bench seating looks more post war and two oblong tables are possibly of oak. To the rear left is a small room with a 1930s brick fireplace. The bar counter continues in an island style but much of it was added in recent years. A room to the right of the passage has a Victorian fireplace with inlaid marble and a fine fender. Live music last Fri. of the month and the pub holds a beer festival in October. In summer open all day. In winter open lunchtimes and evenings.

The fine public bar back fitting at the Star, Talybont-on-Usk, with its mirrored panels and a drawer all of which look to date from around 1930.

Ystradgynlais
108 Brecon Road (B4599) SA9 1QL
01639 843319
Not listed
🚌 120/125 from Swansea (change Pontadawe), X63 Swansea–Brecon
Meals planned

Jeffreys Arms

Large three-storey pub of brick with 'brewers' Tudor' on the second floor built around 1908 with an intact public bar. Double doors on the left lead to the public bar with original counter, original bar back, and has three 'Public Bar' (one a replacement), a 'Jeffreys', and 'Arms' etched front windows, an original fireplace at the rear, and some dado panelling. The counter has a modern Formica top and there is no fixed seating (removed?). The lounge on the right was two small rooms converted into one in the 1970s when the bar fittings were installed. It retains two 'Smoke Room' and a 'Jeffreys Arms' etched windows. The function room on the first floor has 1960s bar fittings and more etched windows – two 'Club Room' and a 'Jeffreys Arms' one. Open at 6pm Mon., Tue., and Wed.; open all day Thu. to Sun. In winter closed all day Mon.

The original bar fittings of the Jeffreys Arms, Ystradgynlais, including a back fitting of four bays, one of which is a walk through for staff to the lounge bar.

POWYS – MONTGOMERYSHIRE/POWYS – SIR DREFALDWYN

Carno
On A470 at the north end of the village SY17 5LH
01686 420206
Grade II listed
🚌 X85 Newtown–Machynlleth*
No food
Guest real ale

**The current bus timetable permits a visit of some 1¼ hours during opening time from the Machynlleth direction only (no suitable return service to Newtown). Check before travelling!*

Ty Brith

A mid 19th century Gothick house, later a country club that became a pub in 1959 and little has changed since. The entrance is at the rear and leads into a hallway where there is an intact off-sales hatch and an open staircase – note the walls have been varnished to look like they have panelling on them. A slatted bar counter with a Formica top and bar back shelves were added in 1959 and serve the two small rooms. Basically furnished, one room has an Edwardian tiled fireplace with a marble surround and green glazed hearth; the other has a 1920s tiled fireplace. Upstairs, but currently not in use, is a snooker room complete with a billiard table and a small bar also installed in 1959. Opens at 4pm Mon. to Sat. Open all day Sun.

When the Ty Brith, Carno, became a pub in 1959 a gap was created between two small rooms and the bar added.

Cemmaes Road/ Glantwymyn
(On A489) SY20 8JZ
01650 511335
Grade II listed
X85 Newtown–Machynlleth
No Accommodation
No food

Dovey Valley Hotel ★

This little-altered small hotel of c.1865–70 is a real step back in time. The entrance to the unchanged public bar is on the right-hand side of the building; hotel guests, many of whom would have arrived by train – the Cambrian line station is across the road, would have entered by the central doorway, which is no longer in use. The unspoilt public bar is a plain room with a three-sided serving area with simple shelving, placed across the innermost corner. This has a counter screen probably dating from the early 20th century with still-working vertical sashes, which were raised and lowered at opening and closing times. The counter front has been covered, presumably around the 1960s, with imitation wood-effect 'beauty board' (an optimistic name if ever there was one!). The disused handpumps still sport the Whitbread Trophy pump clips advertising the beer that once gushed from them. Note the ancient cash register that is currently jammed and has so far defied the efforts of locksmiths! There is an Edwardian tiled fireplace (log fire in winter) with an old 'Worthington's Burton Ales' mirror above. The second, smaller, smoke room lies across the central corridor: it is in occasional use as an overflow from the main bar. It has a lovely old mirror advertising Salt's Burton Ale and signed by the maker, J. Baird of far-away Glasgow.

Unfortunately we couldn't take a photograph of the interior of the Dovey Valley Hotel, Cemmaes Road, so users of the guide will have to go and see how good it is for themselves!

The doors of the main bar and smoke room still carry the numbers '4' and '5' respectively, a survival from the dates when pubs had to have their rooms identified to meet the registration requirements of Customs and Excise authorities. The furniture is a real mixture with much of it suitable for a private living room. But this just serves as a reminder that that's often exactly what public houses were – ordinary houses that doubled up as public places to enjoy a drink. Outside gents' and ladies' (or at least one WC and a separate urinal). As another reminder of times past, note the remnants of the ancient petrol pump on the car park and the adjacent BP cover to access the supply tank. Closed Sun. in winter and usually closed during the day so we strongly recommend you to ring if planning a visit.

Llanfair Caereinion
Parsons Bank SY21 0RR
01938 810759
Not listed
87 from Welshpool (limited service)
Food all day (not Sun. eve) from April to September; Fri. eve, all day Sat. and Sun. lunchtimes in winter
Real ales including Welsh

Black Lion

Early 19th century town pub with a little changed public bar and passageway drinking. A wood-panelled passage runs from the front door to the rear and you will often find locals sitting around the small counter/hatch to the side of the bar. On the left the small quarry-tiled public bar has an old counter and even older wainscoting, however the

The public bar at the Black Lion, Llanfair Caereinion, has a large inglenook featuring a 1930s brick and slate fireplace and high mantel-shelf; the counter front on the right is Victorian and the one on the left is from the inter-war period.

bar back shelving is modern. On the right of the passage the two small rooms were knocked together in 1993 and feature some timber uprights; the front area has a 1930s brick fireplace and some old half-height panelling. A new restaurant has been added upstairs recently and on the front of the pub you will find the smoking shelter, more like another pub room, which even has a log fire! Open all day.

Llanfihangel yng Ngwynfa
SY22 5JD
01691 648209
Not listed
no usable service
No food (There is a tearoom in the village open during the day)

Goat ★

One of the last remaining examples in Wales of a traditional beer house – a domestic property where you can drink in a number of the rooms – still today the 'overspill room' resembles living quarters. The Goat is a rendered house in the middle of the village only distinguished by a pub sign on the side and has been in the same family for four generations. It was originally attached to a dairy and sheep farm, but the land was sold off in 1978. The front door with the figure '1' (a licensing requirement, not part of the pub's address) leads to the original main public room. Originally there were two other small rooms – the 'Bar bach' (small bar) situated to the rear left and another at the end of the passage still with the figure '3' on the door but both of these are now in domestic use only. This follows the decision taken by the present licensee's parents just after they took over in 1956 to convert the room on the right, previously used by the local landowner to collect his rent from tenant farmers, into the public bar. "My parents wanted to concentrate the drinkers in one main room rather than being all over the house"! Despite its closeness to the English border, this part of Montgomeryshire has a strong and vibrant Welsh-language culture.

The original main public room at the Goat, Llanfihangel yng Ngwynfa, looks very domestic and small enough to appear like a hallway. Now acting as the overspill room if the public bar is busy, it has a 1950s tiled fireplace and a piano that is occasionally played.

The public bar at the Goat, Llanfihangel yng Ngwynfa, has a bar counter and bar back shelves installed in c.1956, it already had an old fireplace and is otherwise unchanged with most of the seating consisting of settees, which have to be moved to play darts!

On the second Sunday of the New Year the village holds a plygain service – an unscripted two hours of singing traditional carols in Welsh. Many groups associated with this and related activities use the Goat as a meeting-place so you may find a rehearsal/choir practice here, giving the pub a cultural importance commensurate with its visible heritage. The village's delightful name means "church of St Michael in Paradise". Open evenings from 8pm (possibly before – just knock on the back door!). Although closed lunchtimes it may be possible to arrange a visit between 11 and 3 if you ring to arrange it. Closed all day on Sundays.

Llanfyllin
High Street (A490) SY22 5AQ
01691 648366
www.cainvalleyhotel.co.uk
Grade II listed
🚌 445 from Oswestry, D76 from Welshpool (limited service)
🛏 12 rooms (all en-suite)
Meals lunchtimes and evenings
Welsh or guest real ale

Cain Valley Hotel

17th century former coaching inn, which had a refitting in the 1960s featuring full-height panelling (reputedly from a ship) and the lounge bar and adjoining room are unchanged since. The lounge has a curved wood counter and a bar back from the 1960s. Other items of note are a curved window in the partition wall to the hallway and the narrow door to the servery for staff. To the left the very small dining room also has a heavily carved fireplace – the hatch to the bar is no longer in use. There is a restaurant with half-timbered walls and small 1970s bar. The two-part public bar accessed from Bridge Street was refurbished in 2007. Open all day.

The panelling added to the lounge bar at the Cain Valley Hotel, Llanfyllin in the 1960s is thought to have come from a ship.

The unusual 17th century staircase to the rooms upstairs at the Cain Valley Hotel, Llanfyllin.

Cann Office Hotel

Llangadfan
On A458 SY21 0PL
01938 820202
Grade II listed
🚌 87 from Welshpool (limited service)
🛏 6 rooms (5 en-suite)
Meals lunchtimes and evenings (in winter only Sat. & Sun. lunchtimes and Thu., Fri. and Sat evenings)
Real ale

18th century coaching inn which has retained its original layout of four rooms and is little changed in the last 40 years. Originally part of the Powis Estate and where local farm rents were paid, a further two rooms have been brought into use in recent years. The front right small cocktail bar has a c.1960 bar counter with Formica top. The main tap room on the right has another c.1960 counter and old bare benches. Opposite the servery is what looks like a small hotel reception. Originally the beer was brought from the cellar and served from a hatch to the right of the glass fronted trophy cabinet. Further down the passage is a small bare-boarded room and beyond this a pool room has been brought into use. The front left former lounge is now a modernised dining room and has recently lost its c.1920s ceramic and tile fireplace. There is also a further dining room with no old fittings at the rear. In winter closed Mon. to Wed. lunchtimes.

The quarry-tiled passage of the Cann Office Hotel, Llangadfan, runs from the front door to the rear and has an old counter with old shelves for a bar back.

Crown & Anchor ★

Llanidloes
41 Long Bridge Street (B4518) SY18 6EF
01686 412398
Grade II listed
🚌 X75 from Shrewsbury, 525 from Aberystwyth
No food
Real ales

This 17th century unspoilt town pub consists of five small rooms, one of which was a haberdashery shop until c.1948. It has been in the same family for 200 years and present licensee Ruby Holmes has been running it since 1965. If you ask Ruby what food she sells she will reply "We're just a boozer"! A corridor with half-height panelling divides the two sides of the pub. The tiny snug on the middle right is the original public bar and retains a c.100 year old bar counter (the top was replaced in the 1980s), old bar back shelving with a mirrored backing, and basic bench seating attached to the partition wall. There is a fine

Old cemented-on lettering on the glazed screen around the snug (the original public bar) at the Crown & Anchor, Llanidloes.

Note the old tiny hatch for service in the timber and glass screen around the rear right 'TV Room' of the Crown & Anchor, Llanidloes. The screen on the passageway side still has a tiny window to let the smoke out (the room had a 1950s tiled fireplace until the 1970s) and old 'Truman's Burton Ales' mirror, but the panelling and seating in this room are modern.

mirror advertising 'Ind Coope Burton Ales'. The ribbed hardboard dado panelling was probably added in the 1950s. The rear left room with '2' on the hatch door still retains old panelling with simple fixed bench seating attached. It also has a tiny sliding window in the glass and timber partition wall to let the smoke out and is home to a pool table. The front left small room has a distinctive 1950s tiled fireplace and modern fixed seating. The main bar has shelves on a ply-panelled wall added in 1948 but the present counter dates from the mid 1980s and the fireplace is modern.

TRY ALSO

Whilst in Llanidloes take a look at the **Angel**, High Street SY18 6BY a former coaching inn dating from 1748 with three rooms, two of which are little changed since the early 1970s. The small lounge on the right has a 'penny bar' added in c.1970 with old pennies on the bar top and all around the sides and top of the opening. The public bar on the left has an old counter that used to run all across the top end of the room and has a bar top from the tin-smith next door; bar back looks c.1970. Grade II listed; 01686 412381; Real ales occasionally including Welsh.

Llanidloes
18 China Street SY18 6AB
01686 412247
www.llanidloes.com/mount_inn
Not listed
X75 from Shrewsbury, 525 from Aberystwyth
9 rooms (all en-suite)
Meals lunchtimes and evenings
Real ale

Mount Inn

The Mount Inn has a superb snug formed by two high-backed settles attached to the beamed ceiling by iron stays in front of a Victorian range fireplace. This half-timbered building is situated at the end of the main street in Llanidloes and not far from its splendid Market Hall. As you enter there is an area laid with diamond shaped panels of stone set on edge where the snug is situated. To the rear is the green terrazzo tiled small public bar with an early 20th century wood surround fireplace (the infill is modern), two old curved benches and four Formica top tables. Whilst the bar fittings were replaced in the early 1970s, there are four carved pokerwork panels of local scenes above the counter, which has lower panels of engravings on Aberllefenni slate from the Braichgoch Quarry in Corris, Gwynedd. A slate plaque on the wall states

The public bar at the Mount Inn, Llanidloes

The superb snug at the Mount Inn, Llanidloes, is an excellent example of how the Welsh pub developed from a single room in a domestic property – see How the Welsh pub has changed (pp. 7–9).

that the artist was A D Woodvine and the engraver was R Whitfield. The games room on the left is the venue for Medieval Welsh history lessons on a Tuesday night attended by some 30 local people. The lounge/dining room on the right has modern fittings.

TRY ALSO

Five miles down the road at Llangurig the **Blue Bell** SY18 6SG (on A44) has exactly the same kind of cosy traditional arrangement as at the Mount Inn. This late 18th century building, which was converted to an inn in the mid or late 19th century, has a pair of old settles facing one another beside a range. One of them has a high back rising wall-like up to the ceiling to create a passage behind. It is situated in the slate floored public bar, which is little altered in 30 or 40 years. There is a smaller bar on the left, pool room at the rear and two small dining rooms – all with modern fittings. Grade II Listed; 01686 440254; www.bluebell-inn.co.uk; Guest real ale.

Llanrhaeadr-ym-Mochnant

Market Square (On B4580)
SY10 0JL
01691 780210
www.wynnstay-arms-hotel.com
Grade II listed
D76 from Welshpool (very restricted service)
7 rooms (all en-suite)
Meals lunchtimes and evenings
Real ales

Wynnstay Arms

A hotel built c.1850 in Gothic style whose public bar had a fine refit in the 1950s and is barely changed since then. In common with a number of hotels in Wales, the public bar has its own entrance down the left hand side of the building and remained separate from the rest of the pub until an archway was cut between both parts, possibly in the 1950s. The public bar has bar fittings from the 1950s, a large stone fireplace with a log fire, an old settle, two very old pieces of bench seating, three old tables and a framed brass relief of a domestic scene. At the rear of the bar is a small quarry-tiled floor pool room. From the front stone porch you walk into a hallway/lounge bar with a bar counter added 30

The Coaching Era In Wales

For a brief period the coaching inns of Wales provided a crucial element of the nation's transport infrastructure. From the middle of the seventeenth century existing inns were spruced up or new ones constructed to provide food, drink and beds for travellers together with teams of fresh horses for stagecoaches and, from the 1780s, the fast mail coaches introduced by the Royal Mail.

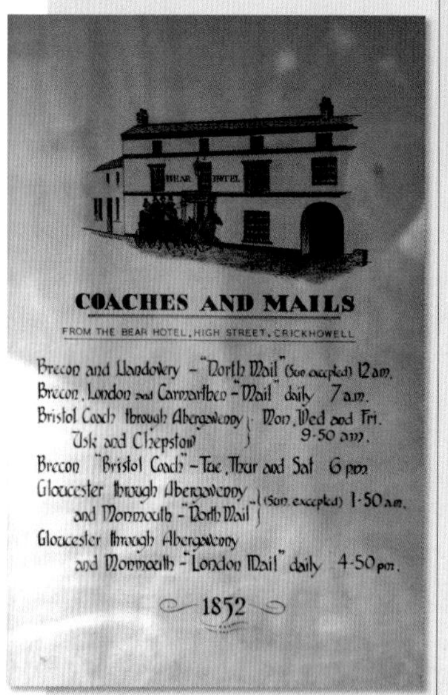

A nineteenth-century stagecoach timetable hangs in the bar of the **Bear**, Crickhowell showing its importance in the coaching era.

The London to Fishguard route saw the development of major coaching inns, with the Angel in Abergavenny converted from a private house to a premier coaching inn in Georgian times, and the Bear at Crickhowell still betraying hints of its former existence, with a fine archway into the inner courtyard.

The snug at the **Blue Bell**, Llangurig (p. 87) has barely changed since its days as a key coaching halt.

In mid Wales the half-timbered Mount Inn in Llanidloes (p. 86) and Blue Bell in Llangurig (p. 87) were key coaching halts, but the Lion Royal Hotel in Rhayader (p. 90) played a crucial role in the development of services in the area once the turnpike road from Kington had been completed in 1779. Within two years the inn, then known as the Red Lion, had its own postchaises and was the terminus for a weekly wagon service which covered the 26 miles to Kington in a mere 12 hours.

All this enterprise was relatively short-lived, however. The 1840s was a decade of abrupt decline as increasing competition from the railways forced the abandonment of many traditional coaching routes. Isolated Rhayader did a little better, but even here the Royal Mail coaches were withdrawn in 1858, and the final stagecoaches ran in 1864, when the railway to Aberystwyth was completed.

Inns such as the **Lion Royal** in Rhayader (p. 90) adapted after the coaching era was over and became country town hotels, serving the new breed of tourists.

The splendid inter-war-style brick and timber bar of the Wynnstay Arms, Llanrhaeadr-ym-Mochnant, was actually installed in the 1950s and still retains its intact glazed shutters, but nowadays the lower ones are always raised.

or so years ago and a passage leads to an old reception hatch. There is another lounge to the right and beyond that are two dining rooms. The gents' has an unusual tiled urinal also dating from the 1950s. In summer open all day. In winter closed Mon. to Thu. lunchtimes.

Welshpool/Y Trallwng
Salop Road SY21 7EZ
01938 553292
Grade II listed
⇌ Welshpool
🚌 X75 Shrewsbury–Llanidloes
No food
Real ale

Grapes

Built in 1835, this is an end of terrace pub with a tiny snug bar barely changed in 100 years whose bar fittings face, unusually, towards the back, not the front of the pub. This remained as a four-room-and-corridor pub until, sadly, the owners decided to "move with the times" (licensee's words) and knock down walls to amalgamate the two left-hand rooms; open the combined room to the corridor; and replace the hatch in the corridor with a new small bar counter. The reason given for these changes is that the pub supports three football teams and there was not enough room for them on a Saturday! The lounge bar at the front probably only came into public use in the 1950s when they cut a hatch into the wall for service to the back of the bar. The small room has a lovely 1950s tiled fireplace and the fixed seating is probably from that date. Outside toilets (under cover) at the rear. Tune sessions last Thu. of the month. Opens at 5.30pm Mon. to Fri.. Open all day Sat. and Sun.

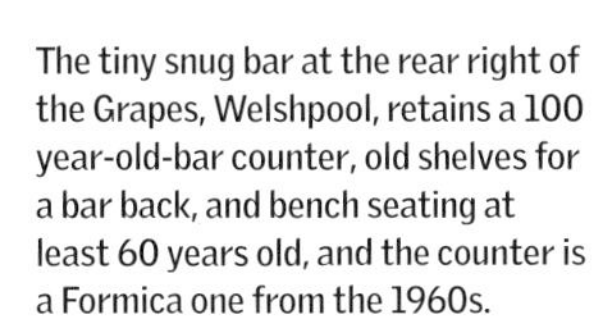

The tiny snug bar at the rear right of the Grapes, Welshpool, retains a 100 year-old-bar counter, old shelves for a bar back, and bench seating at least 60 years old, and the counter is a Formica one from the 1960s.

Church Stoke (Shropshire)
Junction of A489 & B4385 SY15 6SP
01588 620231
Not listed
71 Newtown–Welshpool (limited service)
No food

Blue Bell

Edge-of-the-village traditional pub just a few hundred yards across the border, which has been in the same family ownership since 1926. The public bar was refitted in 1949 and nothing has changed since. The door to the public bar is the original front door – the front lobby was added in 1969. A former stable to the left was converted into the lounge and has a 1950s over-lapped bar counter with a Formica top, glass shelves on wooden bar back, leatherette bench seating, chairs and Formica top tables – all dating from the 1950s, as do the toilets. Opening either the door to the bar or the lounge sounds a bell to announce your arrival. On the other side of the landlady's private hallway there is a dining room on the right, which is used for meetings or private parties. Note the disused petrol pumps outside this brick and part-rendered pub.

The public bar of the Blue Bell, Church Stoke, with a quarry-tiled floor, a bar counter with Formica top, bar back shelves, a brick fireplace and bare oak seating, all from a refitting in 1949.

POWYS – RADNORSHIRE/POWYS – SIR FAESYFED

Rhayader/Rhaeadr Gwy
West Street LD6 5AB
01597 810202
www.lionroyal.co.uk
Not listed
47 from Llandrindod Wells
16 rooms (14 en-suite)
Meals for residents only

Lion Royal Hotel ☆

This unashamedly old-fashioned coaching inn retains a small bar that is unchanged since 1921. Amazingly, stabling for 6 horses and a ¾ acre paddock are still in use today as this is a base for horse riding holidays (British Horse Society approved) from May to the beginning of October and you can bring your own horse or use one owned by the hotel. The hotel has been used as a courtroom, the seat of the Customs and Excise and in 1904 the inaugural meeting of the Royal Welsh Agricultural Society was held here. The present owner recently celebrated 50 years running this hotel, which was until 1904 called the Red Lion and is at least 200 years old. Head for the rear of the hotel and you will find a

The small square public bar of the Lion Royal Hotel, Rhayader, at the rear of the hotel was last refitted in 1921, the date on the Gaskell & Chambers handpumps, and nothing has changed since.

The glazed screen in the passage at the Lion Royal Hotel, Rhayader, includes three sets of sliding screens with etchings of lion's heads on them; one has 'Enquiry' on it.

small square hotel bar with 'Bar' in an etched and frosted panel on the door, a wood-block floor, a wonderful bar counter with Jacobean detailing in the woodwork frontage, two sets of bar back shelves at right angles to each other, one with a mirrored back, a display of 'Gin', 'Brandy' and 'Rum' ceramic spirit vessels, a row of pewter mugs etc. on the shelves, even the ancient 'National' cash register is still in use. The bar fittings appear all of a piece and along with the glazed brick and marble/polished stone fireplace and two sections of bench seating almost certainly do date from the 1920s. An extension to the rear of the bar houses a parquet floor small room no longer in use. Note the bell-pushes labelled 'Chambermaids' and 'Boots' – the latter referring to having your boots cleaned overnight and placed outside your door by first thing in the morning! This service ceased in the 1950s but the bell pushes are still in working order. The lounge in the front left of the hotel has a large stone fireplace with a splendid cast-iron fireback weighing 2¼ cwt., a carved settle, and a light oak bar counter by a local craftsman which was installed in 1969 – hence the crown and Prince of Wales feathers as well as the lion head symbols on it. The bar is only usually open at weekends or when there are groups of people stopping at the hotel – Welsh real ale can be ordered by your party. If you are planning a visit to take a look at the unspoilt bar you are recommended to ring ahead to check when it may be open.

The **Royal Oak** in East Street, Rhayader was in the same family for over 100 years until the death of the last landlord in 2002. Sadly when it reopened after a period of closure it was opened up; however it does retain a rare pewter bar top, the only one we are aware of in the whole of Wales. Real ale.

TRY ALSO

On the outskirts of Rhayader in the district known as Cwmdauddwr is the attractive tucked-away partially timber-clad (possibly 17th century) **Triangle Inn** (off B4518) LD6 5AR. Although altered inside, there are three small distinct places to drink including the lobby inside the front door facing the servery. This tiny area has some wall benches attached to old tongue-and-grooved dado panelling and a counter that looks like the work of c.1960. For the most interesting feature look for the trap door in the left-hand room which reveals a shallow square pit for darts players to stand in. Without this, due to the low ceiling, the darts would hit the beams! Another curiosity is the loos – not just outside, but actually across the road. Has a self-catering cottage that sleeps 3. The village of Cwmdauddwr holds a carol service in the pub. 01597 810537; www.triangleinn.co.uk; Real ales.

Whitney-on-Wye (Herefordshire)
Off A438 HR3 6EU
01497 831262
www.rhydspence-inn.co.uk
Grade II listed
no usable service
7 rooms (all en-suite)
Meals lunchtimes and evenings
Real ales

Rhydspence Inn

A food-led 16th century pub still retaining lots of small characterful rooms. The splendid timber-framed entrance porch is of a style seen only in the Welsh border area – the Welsh/English border is the insignificant brook that trickles through the garden. There is a room above the porch and an externally accessed open gallery. The original bar on the right was revamped c.1960 which is the date of the bar counter. The servery remains in its original position, but bar back shelves date from the 1980s. There are a number of other characterful rooms including one converted from the former kitchen etc. Look for the old coach jack in the hall from the pub's days as a coaching inn.

The rear lounge bar of the Rhydspence Inn, Whitney-on-Wye, was created in c.1960 from former living quarters.

RHONDDA CYNON TAFF/RHONDDA CYNON TAF

Gilfach Goch
Hendreforgan, off A4093
(OS 988875) CF39 8YL
01443 672247
Not listed
150 from Pontypridd, 172 Aberdare–Porthcawl and walk ½ mile
No food
Real ale

Right: The public bar at the Griffin, Gilfach Goch, has a Victorian counter and bar back, a hatch facing the former kitchen part with a red-Formica shelf, a stone fireplace, old benches and a carved settle.

This splendid old till at the Griffin, Gilfach Goch, may date back to 1870 – at the top is a slot for guineas. There is a lever at the top that moves from side to side and as it does it rings a bell. Through a glass panel you can see the guineas as they roll from side to side down into a drawer.

Griffin 'The Bog'

Behind the modern front extension you will find two bars with Victorian fittings and a till dating back to c.1870 with a special slot for guineas. A tucked away pub – it is just off the A4093 and if travelling from the Cardiff direction look for the bus stop just after the village sign and turn left, then drive down a road between modern housing to find it in the valley bottom. Its remote location is due to the existence of an exploratory coal shaft close by as well as the railway running through the valley so the coal board applied for a license on a building they owned. Built in 1881, it has been in the same family since 1961. Walk into a tiny bar still with its old bar back featuring a glass panel in the centre; original counter, dado panelling and a heavily carved settle. A door with the figure '5' on it leads to the public bar, which is an L-shaped room and incorporates part of a former kitchen. There is also a lounge (now games room) on the left side of the pub. The toilet block on the front was added in the early 1960s and a skittle alley above the pub was converted into a flat in 1995, otherwise little has changed. Closed Mon. to Fri. lunchtimes.

Architectural Style in Welsh Pubs

Until the early 19th-century, beerhouses and the public houses – unlike inns – tended to be fairly simple affairs. From c.1890 there was a massive growth in the building of purpose-built public houses, often on a grand scale. Although the majority of these once multi-roomed pubs have been much modernised there are still a number of good examples remaining in Wales that retain a good portion of their original floorplan and quality fittings.

Stunning bar back fittings can be found at the Halfway House, Llanelli (p. 35), the Royal Hotel, Trealaw (p. 98); and in Cardiff the Royal Oak, Adamsdown (p. 20); and the Gower, Cathays (p. 22).

The colourful faience exterior of the **Golden Cross**, Cardiff (p. 23) gives you a foretaste of what to expect inside.

The **Halfway House**, Llanelli (p. 35) retains one of the most impressive remaining Victorian bar fittings.

The Golden Age of Pub Building

Wales is fortunate to have retained two of the most grand of Victorian/Edwardian pub designs involving colourful ceramic tiling. The Golden Cross, Cardiff (1903) (p. 23) has a stunning display of both exterior and interior tiling including a ceramic bar counter and two tiled paintings. The Waterloo Hotel & Bistro, Newport (p. 69) also has a ceramic bar counter and both retain their original mahogany bar fittings.

Good Edwardian fittings can be found at the Capel, Gilfach Fargoed (1912) (p. 17); in two fine red brick Edwardian pubs near Neath, the Ivy Bush, Pontardawe (p. 66) and the Red Cow, Ystalyfera (p. 67). The small public bar at the Lion Royal Hotel, Rhayader was refitted in 1912 (p. 90).

Inter-war pubs

Sadly, we have found few pubs from the inter-war period that have retained their interior fittings and layout. However, Wales has one of the few virtually intact examples in the whole of the UK –

The pictorial windows at **Twthill Vaults**, Caernarfon (p. 55), are examples of 1930s fittings.

The interior of the **Griffin**, Gresford (p. 110) – one of the earliest examples of pub opening-up dating from 1947 featuring segmental archways on solid pillars using polished Ruabon pressed bricks.

the Albion, Conwy (1921) (p. 41) which we recommend is included on a visit to this splendid town. Remains of inter-war re-fits of Victorian pubs are also rare with the Oak Room at the Claude, Roath, Cardiff (p. 21) being a good example. Bangor Station Bar (p. 53) was refitted in 1927. Other 1930s fittings can be seen at Twthill Vaults Caernarfon (p. 55); George & Dragon, Brymbo (p. 109) and the Red Lion, Cyffylliog (p. 46) – the Art Deco toilets are rare.

Post-war pubs

We have not been able to include any new builds from the 1950/60s that are still in original form, as most appear to have been refitted. The Ridgway, Newport (1966) has a distinct style and still has two rooms but was built with three. If you come across any please let us know at info.pubheritage@camra.org.uk

A good example of a 1950s refit based on a 1930s style can be found at the Wynnstay Arms, Llanrhaeadr-ym-Mochnant (p. 87) with its rare screened bar counter.

For two unique re-fittings from the 1950s visit the Pen-y-Gwryd Hotel (p. 57) to see its log bar based on Austrian design and the lounge at the Royal Oak, Llanfarian (p. 112); an even more amazing example is the White Hart, Machen (p. 18), dating from 1961 but using fittings from the 1947 refurbishment of the liner SS Empress of France. The lounge bar at the Old Vigour, Cemaes Bay (p. 12) is an example of how pubs were refitted in the 1960s.

White Horse, Overton-on-Dee.

Refurbishments

Most refurbishments take little note of the original plan form and fittings but the recent work at the White Horse Inn, Overton-on-Dee did return the interior of this Grade II listed pub to close to its original form by the addition of partitions/ screens. It was highly commended in the Best Refurbishment category of CAMRA's Pub Design Awards. Another example of quality modern refitting is the Tudor-style example carried out in c.1990 at the Corvus Inn, St Clears, Carmarthenshire.

Penderyn
54 Chapel Road CF44 9JX
01685 811357
Not listed
7 from Aberdare
No food

Lamb

Traditional drinkers' pub still with three simply furnished rooms and an off sales hatch to the passageway. The sliding sashes still work and the off sales is still in use, mainly by children for sweets; also some customers use it for passageway drinking – note the shelves on the walls used by drinkers. In the wake of the 1831 Merthyr Rising, Richard Lewis, known as Dic Penderyn, was incarcerated in the cellar of the Lamb before being hanged at Cardiff for wounding one of the soldiers brought in to suppress the rising. It is now accepted that he was innocent of this crime. His last words from the scaffold were "O Arglwydd, dyma gamwedd" ("O Lord, here is injustice"). In 1830 the pub was extended and the front door changed to the present one facing the main road. On the left with '1' on the door is the public bar where the counter top has an obvious slope and the red leatherette benches date from the 1960s. The lounge on the right has '4' on the door, Formica top tables and a bench from the 1960s. A stone flagged corridor runs to the rear with a Victorian service hatch for both off sales and use by lounge customers. Behind the public bar is the snug with '2' on the door, a stone flagged floor, fixed bare benches and a tiny hatch to the servery. Used as an office in recent years, this could be back in pub use by now. The door with '3' on it at the rear left is now a private room. Outside gents'. Open all day.

The stone flagged public bar at the Lamb, Penderyn, where panels were added to the front of an old counter in the 1980s. The bar back shelves were built in c.1965 by a previous landlord's son, who was good at woodwork at school!

In Penderyn the **Red Lion**, Church Road CF44 9JR is much changed since 1978 when they installed a bar counter for the first time, but retains old fittings including a high backed settle with iron stay to the ceiling, which forms a short passage from the front door; an old stone fireplace; and a 1920s bentwood bench. 01685 811914. Real ales.

Llanover Arms

Pontypridd
Bridge Street (by slip road to the A470 north) CF37 4PE
01443 403215
Not listed
Pontypridd (rail)
X4 Cardiff–Merthyr (bus)
No food
Real ales regularly including one Welsh; Real Welsh draught cider usually available

Traditional three-roomed drinkers' pub with a fine Victorian bar back fitting in the public bar and hatch service to another room. The basic lino tiled public bar has an interestingly detailed Victorian bar back, an attractive Edwardian Bass mirror and some ancient bench seating. Note the cast-iron tables inscribed 'Gaskells Barfitter Cardiff'; however the bar counter was installed in the mid 1970s. Walk along the panelled corridor through the middle of the pub and on the rear right the L-shaped back room has an over 100-year-old 'Dunville's Whisky' mirror; and a probably 1920s 'Worthington' mirror. The third room with a modern floor sadly lost its wall in the early 1980s so is opened-up to the corridor. Outside gents with all-over terrazzo up to waist height. Dating from c.1790, the pub has an old mounting block on the right hand side; at the rear in the former barn is a steak house restaurant with an upstairs bar, which is run as a separate business and open from 7 to 12 Thu. (1 Fri., Sat., 12 Sun.). Pub open all day.

The rear room of the Llanover Arms, Pontypridd, is served from a hatch with a sliding sash window; also from the stable door to the back of the bar. The brick fireplace may possibly date from the inter-war years.

TRY ALSO

The 17th century **Brynffynnon Inn**, Llanwonno CF37 3PH situated on a wooded hillside five miles north west of Pontypridd is worth a visit to see the public bar on the left. It has an excellent old bar back with arches and mirrors that runs the length of the room. It also retains an old counter but this was shortened many years ago to create access to the toilets. The fireplace is modern. To the right is the lounge, which was once three separate rooms, and has a small modern bar. This isolated pub is popular with walkers, horse riders and cyclists and is open all day. 01443 790272; Welsh real ales.

Trealaw
Brithweunydd Road CF40 2UD
01443 433384
Not listed
Dinas Rhondda
120 Tonypandy–Pontypridd–Caerphilly
No accommodation
Only meals are Sunday lunches
Real ales

Royal Hotel

Large pub built in 1889 and still retaining its splendid original Victorian bar back and counter in the public bar on the right, and a multi-roomed layout. The bar counter is the original (new top) but is shorter than the bar back indicating it has probably been shortened in the recent past. The other public bar fittings include a stone fireplace possibly from the 1960s and modern fixed seating. As you enter the pub there is a large hallway with a hatch for service, originally to the front left room. In the late 1970s this was converted into the Mary Rose Ship Bar, now a dining room created to look like the interior of a ship with slanting walls, bare wood floor, also a boat-shaped bar counter front and stained glass windows created by the licensees at the time. The rear lounge, originally three small rooms, was last revamped in 2007. Opens at 7pm Mon. to Thu.; open 11 am to 2am Fri. and Sat.

The splendid six double bay mahogany back fitting in the public bar of the Royal Hotel, Trealaw, with slender mirror panels and decorative carvings at the top. On the right-hand curved section there is a hatch with intact windows that served one of the rear rooms. It is good to see only a small section of the lower shelves lost for the insertion of a fridge.

Wattstown
Aberllechau Road CF39 0PB
01443 730228
Grade II listed
🚌 132/X32 from Cardiff and Pontypridd
No accommodation
No food

Wattstown Hotel 'Tommy John's'

This is one of the few remaining large late 19th century pubs in the south Wales valleys that have escaped serious modernisation. A visit to the Wattstown Hotel is recommended to see a little-altered snug and passageway drinking rarely seen today. This solid three-storey building of 1892, licensed in 1904, was used as a mortuary following the mining disaster in the National Colliery at Wattstown on 11th July 1905. As you walk in you can usually find some locals drinking in the wide passage with a lino floor and service from a hatch still with sliding windows but with minor 1960s changes. The front right-hand lounge has modern seating and the rear right room is now used for storage. The large L-shaped public bar on the left was at least two rooms in the past and renovated in the 1960s or 1970s with bench seating around the walls and plain bar fittings from that date. Upstairs there are two function rooms which the licensee is trying to bring back into use, one was used as a Buffs lodge. Opens at 1pm (12 Sat., Sun.).

The little-altered smoke room at the Wattstown Hotel, Wattstown is served via a small hatch with a Formica top and front that looks to have been converted from a doorway in the 1960s. The small room has red leather banquette seating around the walls, a tiled & wood surround fireplace and there is a row of "clerestory" windows at the top of the wooden partition wall to the back of the bar.

TRY ALSO

In Llantrisant the **Wheatsheaf Inn**, 28 High Street CF72 8BQ is a four-roomed Victorian pub recently modernised by Celt Experience. It retains a Victorian counter in the small public bar but the old bar back has been replaced. On the far left is a small room and in the passage note the hatch to the side of the bar. The rear room has been modernised and on the right is a dining room. The pub is easy to spot with 'The Wheat Sheaf Hotel' in relief on the bright yellow frontage but difficult to park so head for the village hall car park, a short walk away. Live music Fri. and Sat. nights. 01443 222249; www.wheatsheafllantrisant.com; Welsh real ale.

Lost Pubs

Many of the pubs in this book are small, old-fashioned and facing an uncertain future. A number of such pubs have, however, failed even to come this far, their passing mourned by locals and by connoisseurs of unspoilt and traditional pubs.

Fountain Inn at Troedrhiwgwair lies decaying at the bottom of a narrow lane.

The Fountain

A classic example is the Fountain at Troedrhiwgwair, high in the South Wales Valleys, which originated as a farmhouse but was also in use as an inn by the 1860s. By 1871 the building was known as the Fountain Inn and was owned by Isaac Mason, ancestor of the redoubtable Marge Mason, who ran the pub for many years but died around 2000, since when the pub has been closed.

As you entered the Fountain there was an off-sales window, with the bar in front of you through stable doors and on the left up a green painted slope with lino floor was the Tap Room. To the right was a remarkable survival – the meeting room for the Royal & Ancient Order of Buffaloes, a friendly society which acted as the glue binding together local communities, providing sickness and unemployment benefits and even the funds for a decent burial.

The Ship at Pennant

A similar fate befell the Ship Inn at Pennant, south of Aberystwyth, once described as more a living museum than a pub, largely as a result of the huge collection of bric-a-brac assembled by long-serving landlady Mrs. Pegi Evans, who is quoted as saying that she kept the place as it was in the old days because a pub should be a place 'for the lads from the farms to have peace and quiet to sit and chat.' By the early 1990s Pegi had retired, taking her remarkable collection with her. However the pub continued to trade successfully, with a large extension built onto the drinking area, though the core of the pub retained its character. In 2003, however, the pub was offered for sale by a local estate agent, and in February 2009 retrospective planning consent was eventually granted for 'retention of public house as residential accommodation'.

Use it or Lose it!

It is of course no secret that pubs today are facing difficult trading conditions. When you read this book, please remember that the pubs within it are not just there to be read about – they are there to be *used*! The more that customers use them, the less likely they are to go the way of the much-loved Ship Inn and the Fountain, and countless others that have been lost over the years – and indeed are still being lost, like the New Dock Tavern in Cardiff, closed by Brains in 2009.

New Dock Tavern, Adamsdown, Cardiff – now converted to student flats.

SWANSEA/ABERTAWE

The Mumbles/ Y Mwmbwis
Mumbles Pier SA3 4EN
01792 365230/365225
www.mumbles-pier.co.uk
Not listed
2B from Swansea
Snacks
Occasional real ale

Pier Hotel (Salty Bar & Toby Bar)

Beyond the 1960s extension are two bars retaining 1930s and some 1960s fittings. However, visit it soon as it faces demolition as part of a hotel redevelopment. In the left-hand 'Toby Bar' there is a set of photos of the bars, which were probably taken just after the refit. These show that the Toby Bar is little-altered with the only changes being some padded sections added to the counter front and shelves removed from the bar back; the counter has a copper top and the fireplace remains but with a new fire. The old photos show 1930s panelling on the left hand wall of the Salty Bar, but this has been replaced by 1950/60s panelling. The photos also show a room with a tiny bar counter – where was this – could it be a cocktail or residents bar in the hotel part of the building? The illuminated 'Gents' and 'Ladies' signs over the doors are very 1930s. Part of The Mumbles Pier site, pay the car park fee and get back up to two hours charge off your purchase at the bar. Note the one-way system exit is via a steep hill. Opening hours in school holidays are 12 to 10 daily; in term time open Wed., Thu. 2 to 6; Fri. 2 to 10; Sat., Sun. 12 to 10; Closed Mon., Tue in term-time.

There are a number of colourful leaded panels in the front windows and doors of the Pier Hotel (Salty Bar & Toby Bar), The Mumbles.

The Salty Bar on the right of the Pier Hotel, The Mumbles, retains a splendid pre-war mirrored bar back with a set of drawers and the bar counter appears to date from the early 1960s.

Swansea City Centre/ Canol Dinas Abertawe
56 Wind Street SA1 1EG
01792 456110
Grade II listed
Swansea
all to city centre
Meals 12 to 9 Mon. to Thu.; 12 to 7 Fri., Sat.; 12 to 5 Sun.
Welsh real ale

No Sign Bar

This is by far the most interesting historic pub in Swansea and was frequented by the young Dylan Thomas, one of Wales's most famous poets. Its origins are said to go back several centuries but the modern history of the building dates from the foundation of Munday's, a firm of wine merchants established in 1837 and which came to own many premises in Swansea. Here they had a wine shop, two bars and cellars all of which have left traces today and if you visit at a quiet time you can take a look around and see how a Victorian Wine Merchants operated. The pub now stretches back far to the rear where there is an apparently imported bar counter and on the first floor is Munday's Bar, open at weekends and for private functions. It is said that the unusual name is because the drinking room at the back of the shop was unadvertised. Salubrious Passage appeared in Thomas's story *The Followers* renamed Paradise Passage – the nearby Dylan Thomas Centre in the 18th century former Guildhall celebrates his life and achievements. Open all day.

The front part of the No Sign Bar, Swansea, was Munday's wine merchants shop and beyond the remaining third of a glazed screen and cast-iron columns that divided the shop from the drinking premises behind there are two separate old bar counters, which were no doubt in two separate rooms originally, and an old glass-fronted display cabinet. Entrance to these was from Salubrious Passage to the left of the building beyond the present, adjoining shop.

The cellars of the No Sign Bar, Swansea, with two parallel brick-arched areas divided by an arcade of cast-iron columns probably date back 200 years. The gantry crane on rails that would have been used to hoist and move heavy casks of sherry, port or whatever liquor Munday's were holding is an extraordinary survival. The cellars are now 'The Vault', a live music venue open at weekends.

Upper Killay
553 Gower Road SA2 7DS
01792 203946
Not listed
🚌 18/118 from Swansea
No food
Welsh real ale

Railway

A three rooms and passageway pub in the same ownership as the tiny Swansea Brewery enabling drinkers to sample a number of their beers in unspoilt surroundings. Built in 1864 at the same time as the railway (now a cycle track) that runs alongside it. The small public bar on the left has a bar counter at least 50 years old with a new top, ply-panelled walls from c.1960 and fixed seating of a similar date with the spindly ornamental timbering added later. There are a number of shelves of varying date forming a bar back. Across the passage is a small room that has lost a fireplace and has been brought into use at some time. At the rear is a lounge – originally it was half its present size but it has expanded into domestic quarters in recent years and also has added timbering. The small counter here is a modern addition replacing a hatch – there are no fittings of any great age in this room. Outside gents' and ladies' toilets. Open all day.

The passageway at the Railway, Upper Killay, connects its three rooms and the hatch/door in a part-glazed partition could have been the off-sales in the past.

TORFAEN

Abersychan
Cwmavon Road NP4 8PP
01495 773256
Not listed
🚌 23/24/30/X24 from Newport
Meals all day from Tue. to Sun.
Welsh real ales

Rising Sun

Formerly three cottages, this food-led pub has evolved from a small public bar and now comprises three rooms including the original bar little changed for 50 years. This characterful room has a large inglenook fireplace including a bread oven and old fixed seating down one side of the room. The only change appears to be the adding of some wooden inlay to the seating some 30 years ago. In the 1960s the pub extended into another cottage to create the lounge and into the third cottage in the 1970s hence the two-part room we see today. More recently a dining room has been built onto the side. Open all day. Closed Mon. lunchtimes.

The public bar counter and back fitting at the Rising Sun, Abersychan, were added in the 1950s.

Architectural Ceramics in Pubs

The late Victorian period saw a wide range of decorative and colourful materials used in pub building. Here we indicate where some of the finest remaining examples can be found in Wales.

Faience, being a multi-coloured glazed version of terracotta, gave the exteriors of Victorian and Edwardian pubs an impressive look. The best remaining examples can be found on the exteriors of three pubs in Cardiff city centre – the Golden Cross (p. 23), the Vulcan and the Queens Vaults; also on the Varsity (was White Horse), Aberystwyth, which features 'Rea's' in raised lettering on the fascia. Mr. Rea was the last coachman on the Aberystwyth run in the coaching era.

Glazed tiles were particularly well suited for lining pub walls, being hard wearing and easily cleaned. Occasionally, large tile pictures were commissioned for pubs and inside the Golden Cross, Cardiff (p. 23) there are two hand-painted pictorial panels – in the public bar is one depicting Cardiff Castle in 1903 and in the small side room on the left is one of the Old Town Hall in 1863; both of these are dated 1903 and are by Craven Dunnill of Jackfield, Shropshire. However, the most eye-catching ceramic feature at the Golden Cross is the bar counter, one of only 20 remaining left in the whole of the UK. Wales has another – at the Waterloo Hotel & Bistro, Newport (p. 69).

Floors were also subject to lavish treatment, as the colourful tiled floor at the Castle, Barry (p. 105) shows. Mosaic was another popular material for floors, particularly at the entrance lobbies and in hallways – at the Witchill, Barry (p. 106) it is still visible in the exterior lobby but the hallway is covered over by carpet. At the Kings Arms, Llandudno mosaic was the material used to produce a stunning frontage. In the inter-war period the amount of decoration was much reduced but the Albion, Conwy (p. 41), built in 1921, has a dado of brown tiles with Art Nouveau styling.

The **Golden Cross**, Cardiff (p. 23) has tiled walls, a ceramic bar counter and a tiled painting.

The colourful faience exterior of the **Queens Vaults**, Cardiff (p. 26)

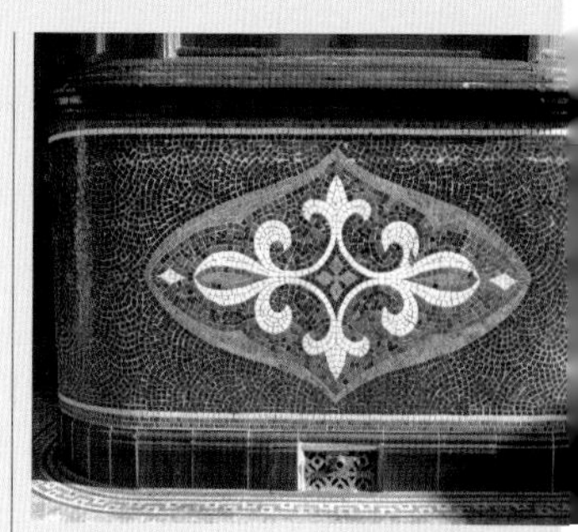

The mosaic frontage of the **Kings Arms**, Llandudno.

The **Castle**, Barry (p. 105) has a colourful tiled floor.

Abersychan
Broad Street NP4 7BQ
01495 774412
Not listed
🚌 23/24/30/X24 from Newport
No Food
Real ale regularly Welsh

White Hart

A multi-roomed drinkers' pub last refurbished in the early 1960s. The public bar on the left is unchanged since c.1960 with ply panelling around the servery, which has some old shelves, bar counter (new top), and fixed seating also possibly from the 1960s. The lounge at the rear also has 1960s fittings – bar counter with a copper top, more ply panelling, stone fireplace etc. The lounge is opened-up to a pool area on the right. A room on the front right with '3' on the door is now used for storage. At the rear right is a room with a removable skittle alley and underneath the pub is a function room where bands play regularly. Open all day.

The passageway from the front door of the White Hart, Abersychan, still retains the original off sales hatch in a part glazed partition complete with window and old wooden shelf.

TRY ALSO

Close by is the **Twyn-y-Ffrwd**, Broad Street NP4 8PJ a three-roomed pub worth a visit. At the front left is a lounge bar with a 1950s brick fireplace and curved counter, difficult to date, with a new top. A short passage to the right leads to a small pool room served by a hatch with c.1960 changes. At the rear is the small public bar on a lower level, which looks like it was last refitted in the 1970s. 01495 775544; Real ale.

VALE OF GLAMORGAN/BRO MORGANNWG

Barry/Y Barri
44 Jewel Street CF63 3NQ
01446 408916
www.sabrain.com/castle-barry
Not listed
🚆 Barry Dock
🚌 88 from Penarth
Meals Mon. to Sat. early evening, Sun. lunchtimes
Brains real ale and guest beers

Castle

Three-storey former hotel built 1898, now a community pub retaining a number of rooms including a former Coffee & Tea Room now housing a full sized snooker table. From the public bar on the left a stone staircase leads down to the basement where there is a skittle alley. On the right the lounge is a combination of the hotel reception at the rear, with the staircase to the bedrooms, and the former Commercial Room (the name is in a window), which has good ceiling roses, The counter at the rear and the bar back with its slender columns and decorative capitals do look original, but the counter to the front dates from the 1960s – the superstructure is definitely modern. The billiard room is down a passage with a colourful Victorian tiled floor – cost to play on the full sized snooker table is only 20p for 15 minutes of light – great value for any budding Terry Griffiths or Mark Williams. The former kitchen with its old range fireplace is now a small dining room. Live bands Fri. nights. Open all day.

The public bar on the left of the Castle, Barry, retains its original counter and bar back. Note the small glazed partition on the right of the bar top creating an office area.

Barry/Y Barri
110 Barry Rd CF63 1BD
01446 734869
Not listed
Cadoxton
B3
No accommodation
No food

Witchill Hotel

Victorian corner pub built 1891 with some of the most ornate ceiling decoration in a pub in Wales; it still retains a rare Jug and Bottle Department. The public bar accessed from Herbert Street was originally two rooms and there was an entrance in the middle of the room. The bar back is the original with some new wood and mirrors but another one on the right has been lost; the counter originally went all along the back wall but was shortened in 1962. The lounge, which is only open in the evenings, is accessed from the Barry Road mosaic floored entrance (WH = Witchill Hotel) – the mosaic floor continued throughout the hallway but is now covered by lino tiles. Formerly two rooms, the lounge retains its original bar back with two deep drawers, one used to store cigarettes, and the counter looks original. The rear part has bar fittings that mainly look from the 1960s but parts are older. There is another superb cornice of grapes and leaves and a 'Smoke Room' panel in the inner door. Between the two bars is the intact Jug & Bottle Department with an etched window, a wood and glass partition, two hatches and shelving.
Open all day.

The high ceilinged public bar at the Witchill, Barry, has an impressive cornice featuring malt shovels, casks, and hops; large ceiling roses; impressive arches and shoulders, the latter two with detail picked out in green and purple. For other impressive ceiling decoration see the frieze and ceiling roses at the Halfway House, Llanelli (p. 35); also the bracket over the fireplace at the Slaters Arms, Corris (p. 55).

East Aberthaw/ Aberddawan
On B4265 CF62 3DD
01446 750329
http://blueanchoraberthaw.com
Grade II* listed
🚌 146/X45/X46 Cardiff/ Barry–Llantwit Major
Meals lunchtimes and evenings (not Sun. evening)
Real ales regularly including Welsh
Real draught cider, usually Welsh, always in summer

Blue Anchor

The Blue Anchor is included in this guide as an excellent example of how to successfully expand a genuinely old building by retaining separate room divisions with the result that it is a pub of great character. In the same family ownership for nearly 70 years, this thatched pub has been authoritatively dated to the mid 16th century and has a layout of six rooms around a central bar. However, it has only been like this for just over 40 years, when more of the building was converted into public rooms – the oldest items inside are the settles and 19th century chairs. Prior to the early 1960s it consisted of just two rooms with beer served from barrels on a stillage. The snug at the front has a low stone doorway and ancient ceiling using horsehair. The front lounge has a modern counter and here you can see beams that were replaced following a major fire in 2004. A flat-roofed extension added in the early 1960s created the long bar and two rooms at the rear which have old settles. A restaurant accessed by a staircase at the rear was added in a further extension in 1984. Open all day.

The public bar situated to the right of the main door is the most traditional of the rooms at the Blue Anchor, East Aberthaw, with its flagstone floor, beamed ceiling, old inglenook fireplace and high backed settle; it has been in use for just 40 years.

Pub Room Names in Wales

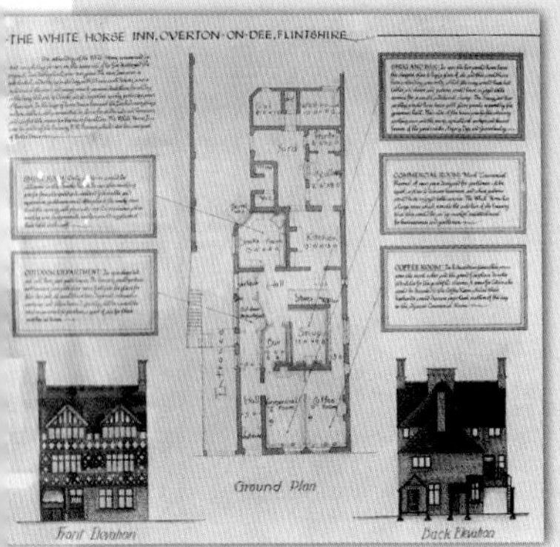

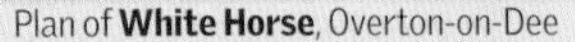

Plan of **White Horse**, Overton-on-Dee

There are a number of good etched windows at the **Capel**, Gilfach Fargoed.

The plan of the White Horse, Overton-on-Dee gives an indication of how pubs were built around 1900; it shows a multi-roomed interior and some of the room names in use then. Today the Public Bar is the most popular name followed by Lounge but often there is little difference in the fittings to distinguish them. In the past the public bar would be the most basic and in some cases offered only standing room. The Lounge or Smoke Room would be much more comfortable and customers would be charged a higher price such as 2d more – something that has virtually disappeared in recent times.

Commercial Room relates to a better class room that would be popular with commercial travellers and other business people on the move. Pubs in this guide still with window glass advertising a 'Commercial Room' include the etched glass ones at Capel, Gilfach Fargoed (p.17) and the Castle Barry (p. 105); also, it is the wording on the door of one of the rooms at the Old Vigour, Cemaes Bay (p. 12).

Another pub with unusual names in glass panels in the doors is the Ystalyfera Arms, Ystalyfera (p. 68) with 'Hall' and 'Smoke Room Glasses Only' ones. Finally, you can see 'Assembly Room' or 'Club Room' – there is one on the first floor of the Jeffreys Arms, Ystradgynlais (p. 80). These are a reminder of how much the pub functions as a social centre.

Numbering the rooms

Close inspection of many pubs will reveal numbers on, over or beside internal doors. The Lamb, Penderyn (p. 96) has '1' on the public bar door; '4' on the lounge on the right; '2' on the snug; and '3' on a room that is now for private use only, which confirms it was in public use in the past. The cellar door at the Sun, Old Colwyn (p. 42) has a figure '3' on it. These numbers were a requirement of H M Customs & Excise.

As well as the Commercial Room wording there is a '4' on this door at the **Old Vigour**, Cemaes Bay (p. 12).

A less common wording is used at the **Royal Oak**, Ystrad Mynach.

These more unusual room names are at the **Castle**, Barry.

Monknash/Yr As Fawr
CF71 7QQ 01656 890209
www.theploughmonknash.com
Grade II listed
145 Bridgend–Llantwit Major
Meals lunchtimes and evenings (not Sun. evening)
Welsh real ales; Real Welsh draught ciders and perry

Plough & Harrow

A 17th century pub with characterful public bar, which is little-altered in 40 years. The main bar on the right was originally two rooms but a partition was removed in the mid 1960s, a staircase to the living quarters was removed and the small bar counter added. The quarry-tiled lounge/dining room on the left has a brick bar and a bar back using old furniture, both added in the mid-1960s. There are two genuinely old fireplaces. Live music Sat. evenings. Runs its own beer festival on the last weekend in July. Open all day.

Up to the mid-1960s a partition attached to the beam on the right of the bar counter separated a narrow snug from the public bar at the Plough & Harrow, Monknash.

WREXHAM/WRECSAM

Brymbo
Ael-y-Bryn LL11 5DA
01978 852231
Not listed
12, 13, 15, 15A, 16A from Wrexham
No food
Lees real ale

George & Dragon

Hidden away three-roomed village pub, which still retains fittings from the 1930s when an extension was added to a much older pub. A doorway to the left of McGill's bar (named in honour of customer Dave Curtis, who resembled McGill, the man in a suitcase) leads to the small public bar. This has an old, at least 1930s, bar counter; but the fireplace and fixed seating look more 1960s, and the bar back was replaced in the 1980s. To the right is the lounge that was two small rooms. It has an interesting carved counter added in the 1970s, possibly to replace a hatch. Fixed seating and the distinctive fireplace look 1960s. Both Gents' and Ladies' have a 1930s panel in the door and inter-war tiles on the walls, as does the porch. Open all day.

At the George & Dragon, Brymbo, the front door leads to a tiny snug called McGill's Bar which has an old, at least 1930s, bar counter painted cream. Take a close look at the door between the bars and you can see it was raised around 9 inches in height (in 2003) to stop customers banging their heads!

Griffin

Gresford
Church Green LL12 8RG
01978 852231
Not listed
🚌 1 Wrexham–Chester
No food
Real ales including a guest beer

This old pub has a most interesting interior – what is possibly one of the earliest examples of the opening-up of a pub interior of four rooms having been undertaken around 1947 by the Chester Northgate Brewery. Opening-up of pubs by the removal of walls is something that happened from the 1960s onwards as the orgy of pub opening, modernisation etc. took place in the country's pubs. The pub is also run on very traditional lines with no food, no piped music, no machines and no pool table (there is a TV, but it is rarely used). Since 1971 it has been run by Jean Williams, an accomplished pianist who will play if requested by the locals, particularly on Fri. & Sat. evenings. Opens at 4pm every day.

One of the four opened-up rooms of the Griffin, Gresford, which has the feel of an earlier period with its good inter-war fixed bench seating.

£50 for the empties but Price won't sell

Look for the empty beer can at the Griffin, Gresford, which is apparently worth more than 'a few bob'!

Ruabon Tiles

Many of the quarry tiles gracing the floors of pubs in Wales and elsewhere came from the Ruabon "Red Works" which was founded in 1878. The famous hard, durable bricks were responsible for many red buildings in and around the Wrexham area. But they were also in great demand across the UK during the late Victorian re-building programme. At Liverpool University, the Victoria Building was constructed in 1892 from Ruabon brick and terracotta. In Cardiff Bay, Ruabon produced the terracotta murals for the side of the Pier Head building. It traded as Dennis Ruabon Tiles Limited, named after founder Henry Dennis, and was the only remaining quarry tile manufacturer in the UK until production ceased in 2008, but it is hoped it may restart.

In 1947 at the **Griffin**, Gresford local builders Richard Randles & Son of Marford created segmental archways with a shallow rise and solid pillars using polished Ruabon pressed bricks with rounded quoins. The two bar counters are of polished Ruabon brickettes laid in a herringbone fashion and they replaced two hatches. There are four fireplaces with differing styles all from c.1950, also using polished Ruabon bricks.

Wrexham/Wrecsam
45-47 Ruabon Road LL13 7PL
01978 261450
Not listed
Wrexham Central
All to Wrexham town centre
Meals lunchtimes and evenings
Marstons real ale

The lounge at the Oak Tree, Wrexham was formerly two small rooms and has fittings from the 1960s. The rear section has a 1950s brick fireplace and a hatch for service.

Oak Tree

The Oak Tree is the least altered pub in Wrexham with three rooms and stables at the rear. The public bar still retains an old vestibule entrance and the bar counter and bar back probably date from the 1960s. On the rear right the games room housed a full sized snooker table until a few years ago but still retains some original fixed seating and modern high backed settles. Open all day.

The nearby **Bowling Green** has the most surviving etched windows in a Wrexham pub – note the 'Bottle & Jug Entrance' in stone above a blocked-up arch. Real ale. A rare survivor is the small thatched historic **Horse & Jockey** in the redeveloped town centre of Wrexham. It still retains a traditional layout but a couple of fires in the 1970/80s unfortunately destroyed any old fittings. Real ales.

Closed Pubs

The following pubs would all have appeared in the body of this book but, regrettably, they were closed as we went to press. We hope they will reopen soon and here we give you a flavour of what to expect if you are able to visit them.

The fireplace in the Elizabethan Lounge of the **Royal Oak**, Llanfarian with its elaborate Jacobean carved surround that came from Tan-y-Bwlch mansion.

Royal Oak, Llanfarian (On A487), Ceredigion SY23 4BS

The real star here is the Elizabethan Lounge on the right. It was expensively fitted out to celebrate the coronation of Queen Elizabeth II in 1953. It has full height panelling all around the room that came from Llanfarian Village Hall and has shields representing the counties of Wales, their meaning and 'their descriptions in heraldry'. It features a 1950s Tudor Arch shaped brick fireplace – the style seen in the days of Elizabeth I, who with Elizabeth II is featured on the plaque above the fireplace. The owner is looking for new tenants. 01970 630411.

Queens Head, Bryndu, near Ty Croes station, Isle of Anglesey LL63 5RW.

A three-roomed pub that was unchanged for many years due to a long serving licensee, Mrs Evans. In the 1990s there was some opening-up but it still retains a splendid front room served via a hatch; it is like someone's sitting room with its settee and armchairs. A separate small room on the left is now opened-up to the passage. A third small room with a pool table has also lost its wall to the passage. Closed and for sale through agents Dafydd Hardy 01407 766828.

Boot & Shoe, 2 Castle Street, Kidwelly, Carmarthenshire SA17 5AX

This is a small pub by the castle gate. The passage from the door with a red-and-black quarry tiled floor has an old shelf and a hatch to the side of the bar. There is a very small quarry tiled floor bar with a row of clerestory windows above the counter being the oldest fittings. On the left the two small rooms were knocked together a few years ago. This Felinfoel tied house is being advertised as 'For Let'.

Glynne Arms, 3 Glynne Way, Hawarden, Flintshire CH5 3NS (B5125)

This early 19th century coaching inn owned by Hawarden Estate closed when the brewery owning the lease went into liquidation. Before it closed it had two small bars that were separate until linked in recent years. There was another bar on the rear right which has 1930s bar fittings. However, the estate have plans for changes before re-opening the pub so let us hope that they preserve the old pub fittings.

Public Transport to the Pubs

When a featured pub is within half a mile from a railway station we say so. We also indicate bus route numbers. In most cases we also give a brief description of the route (e.g. 585 Aberystwyth – Lampeter); if only a bus route number is given, the route starts/terminates in the town or city centre. The quoted routes do not necessarily go right past the pub, but will always stop nearby. While we have tried to include only routes that run when the pub is open, these may nonetheless be infrequent so please check an up-to-date timetable. Wales's 22 counties vary wildly in the standard and availability of their printed timetable information, but their websites are often useful – go to **www.countyname.gov.uk** and follow links. You can also check times with Traveline Cymru on 0871 200 22 33 or **www.travelinecymru.info**. In particular, services on Sundays and public holidays are often shockingly bad – poor even in populous areas, and simply non-existent over large tracts of the country – so it's particularly important to check times for these days. In a few cases, mainly for pubs with restricted opening hours, the entry says 'no usable service'; this means there is no bus when the pub is open, but buses do run at other times (*so you could, for example, at least see the pub's exterior, or satisfy yourself of its location for a future visit*).

If you're spending a few days visiting Welsh pubs, a Freedom of Wales Flexipass is well worth considering. An 8-day All Wales pass, allowing eight days' travel on most scheduled bus routes plus four days' rail travel within the eight (anywhere in Wales bounded by the Chester–Crewe–Shrewsbury–Newport route) costs £78, with a discount for railcard holders. There are also regional passes – one for south Wales, one for north and mid Wales – offering similar availability within their area for £53 each. These also entitle you to discounts or money-saving offers on preserved heritage railways, National Trust, CADW: Welsh Historic Monuments, and other organisations. Full details and booking on 0870 9000 773 or **www.walesflexipass.co.uk**.

There are also a number of one-day multi-journey tickets to save both money and the inconvenience of frequent re-booking. North Wales Rover is a family of zonally based tickets covering trains and buses in the six counties of north Wales (Anglesey, Gwynedd, Conwy, Denbighshire, Flintshire, Wrexham) with extensions south to Aberystwyth and east to Chester. Prices for a day's travel range from £7 for two zones up to £22 for all eight, and tickets are available from railway ticket offices and bus drivers. In Gwynedd and Anglesey (and on some cross-boundary routes e.g. to Llandudno), the Tocyn Coch or Red Rover ticket offers unlimited bus travel for £5.40, while in the south-western counties of Ceredigion, Carmarthenshire, and Pembrokeshire the West Wales Rover buys you travel on almost all bus services for £6.80. In south-east Wales, the Network Rider ticket at £7 covers travel on Cardiff Bus, Newport Bus, Stagecoach, and Veolia along with a number of small independent operators.

A number of operators also offer one-day tickets restricted to their own services. On rail, a Cardiff Valley Lines Day Explorer costs £8.20 and allows travel on the Valley Lines network from Cardiff up the former mining valleys and also down to Barry (you can also use this on Stagecoach and some other buses). Bus operators offering one-day tickets include Arriva at £5.50 (mainly useful for north Wales and Ceredigion), Cardiff Bus at £3 or £4.20 depending on area covered, and First Cymru at £3.90 for the Swansea Bay area or £7 for their entire network, which extends into Carmarthenshire and Pembrokeshire.

Finally, may we recommend one essential piece of equipment before you set out to visit Wales's heritage pubs by public transport (*apart from this book, that is*). Published annually and available free of charge from tourist information centres, the Wales Bus, Rail, and Tourist guide features a comprehensive fold-out route map of Wales's bus and rail routes backed by a description of each route telling you roughly how often they run along with much other useful information. It has proved invaluable in compiling these notes and will undoubtedly make your journeys very much easier.

Please note that prices quoted were the latest available at time of going to press, and in most cases were the prices current at the end of 2009. All prices are subject to change. The prices quoted are for one adult; family versions of most tickets are also available. Finally, although Wales preceded England in offering free local bus travel to senior citizens, regrettably senior citizens' bus passes issued outside Wales are not valid for travel within the country (with certain exceptions for cross-boundary services).

Index

Page numbers in **bold** indicate illustrations

Index

Douglas Arms, Bethesda

Books for beer lovers

CAMRA Books, the publishing arm of the Campaign for Real Ale, is the leading publisher of books on beer and pubs. Key titles include:

Good Beer Guide 2010

Edited by **ROGER PROTZ**

The *Good Beer Guide* is the only guide you will need to find the right pint, in the right place, every time. It's the original and best-selling independent guide to around 4,500 pubs throughout the UK. Now in its 37th year, this annual publication is a comprehensive and informative guide to the best real ale pubs in the UK, researched and written exclusively by CAMRA members and fully updated every year.

£15.99 ISBN 978 1 85249 266 3

London Heritage Pubs – An inside story

GEOFF BRANDWOOD & JANE JEPHCOTE

The definitive guidebook to London's most unspoilt pubs. Raging from gloriously rich Victorian extravaganzas to unspoilt community street-corner locals, these pubs not only have interiors of genuine heritage value, they also have fascinating stories to tell. *London Heritage Pubs – An inside story* is a must for anyone interested in visiting and learning about London's magnificent pubs.

£14.99 ISBN 978 1 85249 247 2

Scotland's True Heritage Pubs

Edited by **MICHAEL SLAUGHTER**

This unique guide will lead you to 115 Scottish pubs which have historic fittings of real national significance, many of which have altered little in the past 40 years or so. Some of the featured pubs are tiny, old-fashioned time-warp inns, others are magnificent Victorian drinking palaces and Art Deco masterpieces. There are also several quirky pubs, including one hidden away in a terrace.

£4.99 ISBN 978 1 85249 242 7

Do you feel passionately about your pint? Then why not join CAMRA

Just fill in the application form (or a photocopy of it) and the Direct Debit form on the next page to receive three months' membership FREE!*

If you wish to join but do not want to pay by Direct Debit, please fill in the application form below and send a cheque, payable to CAMRA, to:

CAMRA, 230 Hatfield Road, St Albans, Hertfordshire AL1 4LW.

Please note that non Direct Debit payments will incur a £2 surcharge. Figures are given below.

Please tick appropriate box	Direct Debit	Non Direct Debit
Single membership (UK & EU)	☐ £20	☐ £22
Concessionary membership (under 26 or 60 and over)	☐ £14	☐ £16
Joint membership	☐ £25	☐ £27
Concessionary joint membership	☐ £17	☐ £19

Life membership information is available on request.

Title ____________ Surname ____________

Forename(s) ____________

Address ____________

____________ Post Code ____________

Date of Birth ____________ E-mail address ____________

Signature ____________

Partner's details (for Joint membership)

Title ____________ Surname ____________

Forename(s) ____________

Date of Birth ____________ E-mail address ____________

CAMRA will occasionally send you e-mails related to your membership. We will also allow your local branch access to your e-mail. If you would like to opt-out of contact from your local branch please tick here ☐ (at no point will your details be released to a third party).

Find out more about CAMRA at www.camra.org.uk *Telephone* **01727 867201**

**Three months free is only available the first time a member pays by Direct Debit*

Instruction to your Bank or Building Society to pay by Direct Debit

DIRECT Debit

Please fill in the form and send to: Campaign for Real Ale Ltd. 230 Hatfield Road, St. Albans, Herts. AL1 4LW

Name and full postal address of your Bank or Building Society

To The Manager — Bank or Building Society

Address

Postcode

Originator's Identification Number

9	2	6	1	2	9

FOR CAMRA OFFICIAL USE ONLY
This is not part of the instruction to your Bank or Building Society

Membership Number

Name

Postcode

Name (s) of Account Holder (s)

Bank or Building Society account number

Branch Sort Code

Reference Number

Instruction to your Bank or Building Society
Please pay CAMRA Direct Debits from the account detailed on this Instruction subject to the safeguards assured by the Direct Debit Guarantee. I understand that this instruction may remain with CAMRA and, if so, will be passed electronically to my Bank/Building Society

Signature(s)

Date

Banks and Building Societies may not accept Direct Debit Instructions for some types of account

detached and retained this section

DIRECT Debit

This Guarantee should be detached and retained by the payer.

The Direct Debit Guarantee

- This Guarantee is offered by all Banks and Building Societies that take part in the Direct Debit Scheme. The efficiency and security of the Scheme is monitored and protected by your own Bank or Building Society.
- If the amounts to be paid or the payment dates change CAMRA will notify you 10 working days in advance of your account being debited or as otherwise agreed.
- If an error is made by CAMRA or your Bank or Building Society, you are guaranteed a full and immediate refund from your branch of the amount paid.
- You can cancel a Direct Debit at any time by writing to your Bank or Building Society. Please also send a copy of your letter to us.